DISON BRASIL

First Year of

GRIEF CLUB

A GIFT FROM A FRIEND WHO GETS IT

FIRST YEAR OF

GRIEF CLUB

A GIFT FROM A FRIEND WHO GETS IT

ADDISON BRASIL

ISBN Hardcover: 978-0-578-36595-4
ISBN Paperback: 978-0-578-36684-5

DEDICATION

To my brother, Austin.
To my father, Henry.
To my beautiful friend, Dee.

Losing each of you forced me into Grief Club
and carved out the deepest darkest sorrow within me.

It also gave me the capacity to search for light,
and to experiment with love, awe and hope.

To my personal champions
and those who invested in me not just surviving,
but thriving with my losses …
the ones who made sure I am here today.
I promised if you got me through,
I would go back for the others.

Here I am.

FIRST YEAR OF

GRIEF CLUB

A GIFT FROM A FRIEND WHO GETS IT

(Not someone who would ever claim to know exactly how you're feeling, but from someone who gets that flowers, condolences, and casseroles are just the beginning.)

" HAVING HAD THE PRIVILEGE OF BECOMING FRIENDS
WITH ADDISON, I CAN CONFIDENTLY SAY THAT FEW
PEOPLE SPEAK ABOUT HEALING GRIEF THROUGH FINDING
MEANINGFUL CONNECTION AND SERVICE AS ELOQUENTLY
AND THOUGHTFULLY AS HE DOES. IN HIS BOOK, HE SHARES
DEEPLY VALUABLE PERSPECTIVES THAT HAVE HELPED ME
FIND THE TOOLS AND APPROACHES TO HEALING THAT I
HAD YET TO UNCOVER PREVIOUSLY. IF YOU OR SOMEONE
YOU KNOW IS SUFFERING, I COULD NOT RECOMMEND
MORE HIGHLY TAKING THE OPPORTUNITY TO IMMERSE
YOURSELF INTO THIS BOOK. "

–ZAK WILLAMS:
Mental Health Advocate, Founder of You Can PYM

" DEATH AND GRIEF ARE UNAVOIDABLE RITES OF
PASSAGE FOR US ALL. IN *FIRST YEAR OF GRIEF CLUB*,
ADDISON BRASIL HAS TAKEN HIS THIRTEEN YEARS OF GRIEF
AND PROVEN THAT RITUALS CREATED AROUND HONORING
ONE'S JOURNEY, NOT TRYING TO FIX IT, CAN LEAD US TO OUR
OWN WISDOM AND TOOLS FOR LOSS. "

–CHIP CONLEY:
New York Times Bestselling Author,
Founder of Modern Elder Academy, and Wisdom Well

" *FIRST YEAR OF GRIEF CLUB* FEELS LIKE HE'S PUTTING
HIS ARM AROUND READERS AND GENTLY GUIDING THEM
THROUGH THE PROFOUND HUMAN JOURNEY THAT IS
GRIEF. SO, PLEASE SKIP THE OVERPRICED FLOWERS AND
UNDERCOOKED CASSEROLES. SEND THIS BOOK TO ANYONE
ENTERING THE GRIEF CLUB! "

–SHELLEY PAXTON:
Author of *Soulbbatical: A Corporate Rebel's Guide to Finding Your Best Life*

"ADDISON HAS CREATED A SAFE SPACE FOR EVERYONE WHO IS GRIEVING TO CALL HOME. HIS EXPERTISE IN THE "GRIEF ARENA," ALONG WITH HIS STORIES OF TRANSFORMATION, TURN INTO AN OPPORTUNITY FOR US ALL TO FIND A WAY THROUGH LOSS THAT WORKS FOR US AS INDIVIDUALS, BUT ALSO CAN BE DONE AS A COMMUNITY. A TRUE INVITATION TO GET TO KNOW YOURSELF WITH COMPASSION AND CURIOSITY AS YOU NAVIGATE GRIEF. ADDISON'S WORDS ARE THE MOST IMPORTANT WORDS WE NEED AT THIS TIME."

–JUSTIN MICHAEL WILLIAMS:
Author, *Stay Woke: A Meditation Guide for the Rest of Us*

"ADDISON BRASIL HAS TAKEN THE DARK MOMENTS OF HIS LIFE AND SHOWN ALL OF US A WAY FORWARD WITH COURAGEOUS CURIOSITY, COMPASSION, AND ABOVE ALL ELSE, KINDNESS TO OURSELVES AND OTHERS WHEN NAVIGATING THE GRIEF AND LOSS THAT ALL OF US MUST NAVIGATE AT ONE POINT."

–HOUSTON KRAFT: Author of *Deep Kindness:*
A Revolutionary Guide for the Way We Think, Talk, and Act in Kindness

"AS A FILMMAKER AND EDUCATOR WHO WORKS WITH SURVIVORS OF VIOLENCE, I HAVE SEEN SO MANY SUFFERING LOSS AND GRIEF, THAT I FELT I LACKED ALL THE TOOLS TO HELP WITH. AND AS A PERSON WHO HAS EXPERIENCED MANY LOSSES OF LOVED ONES THAT I AM JUST NOW COMING TO TERMS WITH, *FIRST YEAR OF GRIEF CLUB* PROVIDES INSIGHTS AND PERSPECTIVES OFFERING GUIDANCE, INSIGHTS, AND PRACTICES, TO HELP SURVIVORS THROUGH THE JOURNEY OF RECOVERY."

–INDRANI PAL-CHAUDHURI:
Director, Photographer, Author of *Icons*

" ADDISON OFFERS THE KIND OF COMFORTING INSIGHT AND HELPFUL PROCESSING EXERCISES THAT ONLY SOMEONE FROM HIS UNFORTUNATE LEVEL OF GRIEF-EXPERIENCE POSSIBLY COULD. THE PAIN WON'T DISAPPEAR, BUT HIS COMPASSION, EMPATHY, AND STRENGTH THROUGH THE PROCESS WILL ALWAYS BE PRESENT FOR YOU, ENCOURAGING YOU, AND HELPING YOU HONOUR THE PROCESS IN YOUR BEST WAY. HIGHLY RECOMMENDED! **"**

–JENIFER MERIFIELD:
Mentor, Coach, Host of Extraordinary Life Podcast

" *FIRST YEAR OF GRIEF CLUB* IS BOTH HIGHLY PERSONAL AND COMPLETELY UNIVERSAL. GRIEF IS A TOPIC ALL OF US DEAL WITH BUT ALMOST NO ONE LIKES TO TALK ABOUT. ADDISON BRASIL'S WRITING REMOVES THE STIGMA THROUGH CREATIVE, ACCESSIBLE AND PRACTICAL EXERCISES THAT LEAVE READERS FEELING LESS ALONE AND MORE A PART OF A COMMUNITY OF HEALING. **"**

–ELEX MICHAELSON:
News Anchor, FOX 11 Los Angeles

" SO MUCH ABOUT THIS BOOK IS EFFECTIVE AND WHAT GRIEVING PEOPLE TRULY NEED — FROM THE GENTLE, PATIENT, EMPATHETIC TONE TO THE CAREFUL MIX OF RESEARCH AND HELPFUL QUOTES TO THE SMALL, DAILY PRACTICES THAT FEEL MANAGEABLE. **"**

–ANDREW REINER:
Author, *Better Boys, Better Men: The New Masculinity That Creates Greater Courage and Emotional Resiliency*

" THERE IS NO RIGHT OR WRONG WAY TO GRIEVE. EVERYONE DOES IT IN THEIR OWN TIME, BUT THIS BOOK CERTAINLY HELPS YOU ALONG THAT JOURNEY. IT OFFERS A LIFE LESSON THAT EVERYONE NEEDS TO LEARN. **"**

–Dr. RANJ SINGH:
Author, Pediatrician and TV Personality

" THIS BOOK IS A GAME-CHANGER IN THE WORLD OF GRIEF. UNLIKE SO MANY BOOKS FULL OF THEORY AND 'ENCOURAGEMENT,' IN *FIRST YEAR OF GRIEF CLUB* ADDISON GENTLY TAKES YOUR HAND AND GUIDES YOU BACK TO YOUR BODY, YOUR HEART, AND YOUR TRUE SELF THROUGH THE SIMPLE PRACTICES OF CURIOSITY AND COMPASSION. I'VE SPENT MY LIFE IN THE WORLD OF LOSS AND GRIEF, BOTH PERSONALLY AND PROFESSIONALLY, AND THIS BOOK IS EXACTLY WHAT YOU NEED TO NAVIGATE THE TENDER DAYS AND EMOTIONS AFTER A DEATH, JOB LOSS, END OF A RELATIONSHIP, OR ANY OTHER LOSS THAT ROCKS YOUR EMOTIONAL WORLD. THIS IS THE BOOK I GIVE TO MY CLIENTS AND LOVED ONES AS SOON AS GRIEF ENTERS THEIR WORLD. **"**

–CATHERINE HAMMOND:
Estate Planning Attorney and Author of *hope(less)*

" SOMEONE ONCE TOLD ME THAT GRIEF IS SIMPLY LEARNING TO LIVE WITH LIFE NEVER BEING THE SAME AGAIN, AND REALIZING THAT DOESN'T MEAN YOUR LIFE IS OVER, IT'S JUST DIFFERENT. EASIER SAID THAN DONE UNLESS YOU HAVE A ROADMAP TO MAKE IT SO. *FIRST YEAR OF GRIEF CLUB* IS THAT ROAD MAP. **"**

–DR. MARK GOUSLTON, M.D:
Co-author, *Why Cope When You Can Heal?*

" THROUGH *FIRST YEAR OF GRIEF CLUB* ADDISON BRASIL OFFERS US A COMFORTING FRIEND, A CONFIDANT, AN EMPATHETIC GUIDE FOR NAVIGATING THE TRICKY WATERS OF GRIEF. WHETHER DEALING WITH A PERSONAL OR PROFESSIONAL LOSS, OR RECKONING WITH THE CHANGES OF A PANDEMIC REALITY WHEREAS HE WRITES – "OUR WAYS OF GRIEVING FORMALLY AND INFORMALLY HAVE SHIFTED," ADDISON BRASIL HANDS US THE BLUEPRINTS FOR MOVING FORWARD. THIS BOOK IS A TOOL FOR CONFRONTING THE COMPLEXITIES AND UNCERTAINTIES OF LIFE AND REALIZING THAT OUR GREATEST STRENGTH FOR ACCEPTING GRIEF COMES FROM WITHIN. **"**

–BRIAN MASTROIANNI:

Widely published health and science

" *FIRST YEAR OF GRIEF CLUB* IS NOT ONLY A HELPFUL RESOURCE FOR THE GRIEVING. IT'S ALSO A THOUGHTFUL GIFT TO SUPPORT A FRIEND OR LOVED-ONE WELL BEYOND CARNATIONS AND CASSEROLES. DELIVERED WITH WARMTH, COMPASSION, AND WISDOM, BRASIL'S BOOK IS A LANTERN IN THE DARK WOODS OF GRIEF. **"**

–DR MANDY LEHTO:

Personal Coach and Host of Enough, the Podcast

" THE MOST IMPORTANT GIFT YOU CAN GIVE A FRIEND IN GRIEF. **"**

–David Vox:

Transformational Teacher

CONSCIOUS CHECK POINT:

In this moment pick one word to describe:

How are you feeling physically?

How are you feeling emotionally?

How are you feeling mentally?

We will always check in before doing any grief experiments or entering the Grief Club arena as peers. It is important to know how you are feeling before approaching anything. The check-ins are here to honour where you are at in the moment. These check-ins don't define you they just help you to make conscious decisions in your grief journey.

TABLE OF CONTENTS

THE SHAME 79

THE SURRENDER 105

PROLOGUE

People say that I have been through impossible experiences. The trauma, the death, and the grief are not something they could ever get through. So naturally, they deem me as strong. It's a beautiful and broken act of self-preservation — to compliment me while simultaneously warning the universe — *this can never happen to me*. But it happens, and whether it's compounded or not, we all end up in the Grief Club arena one day.

The arena is the return on investment of connection. And to connect is what makes us human beings in our simplest forms. If we want to *be* then we silently agree to one day grieve how we got to be, and with who, and when. It's just the way it is.

Even after losing my brother, my father, and my friend I never knew what to offer someone when I heard that they were entering Grief Club. I would find myself in this weird paralysis. I never wanted to make eye contact. I didn't want to let them see my worry, and thereby avoided compassion, empathy, and love twisting into a concerned look, followed by condolences that went sour in my mouth before I even finished speaking or texting. After what I've lived through, people always ask me what they should do for someone who has just experienced a devastating and meaningful loss. The pause I take before answering with some hopeful saying I didn't believe in was one I could no longer reconcile. The pause became a freeze, one that tugged on my soul and not-so-gently asked – *why aren't you showing up in this moment?* This book will fill that space where I didn't know how to show up. This is the, "I heard … and as a friend who gets it, I'm gonna be here with you for the next year."

This is with you, for you.

But it is all going to come down to you. You will ultimately choose how you come out of this. You will choose whether to open back up to love or retreat. You will choose whether you want to get to know the *you* that now exists. You will choose if you want to live within loss or die with the death of what once was. This book is a reminder, whether it sits on your nightstand or coffee table, or gets beaten up in your gym bag, that I hope you choose to continue being. When you see it, touch it, open it — you breathe into the safety of knowing, no matter what you are feeling — it's part of the journey.

This book is for you in the silence, the swirl, the shame, the survivor, the surrender, the show-up. It's a reminder that it's all up to you, and that just opening it up once a week or whenever you can is an act of radical resilience.

Nothing will be fixed by these offerings, but all will be honoured.

This is your journey, and the physical form and space this book takes up in your world is a reminder that in Grief Club, you get to choose to honour it, all of it.

GRIEF IS NOT SOMETHING YOU FIX; IT'S SOMETHING YOU HONOUR.

GRIEF CLUB RULES

THE FIRST RULE OF GRIEF CLUB:
You get to talk about Grief Club as much as you want.

THE SECOND RULE OF GRIEF CLUB:
You get to talk about Grief Club as much as you want.

THE THIRD RULE OF GRIEF CLUB:
The definition of grief is a living, breathing thing,
and only you can define YOUR grief.

THE FOURTH RULE OF GRIEF CLUB:
Allow yourself to build awareness through
weekly experiments and offerings.

THE FIFTH RULE OF GRIEF CLUB:
You can stop when you want, pause,
and come back whenever you want. Membership is for life.

THE SIXTH RULE OF GRIEF CLUB:
Only do what serves you. If awareness leads to action — celebrate.
If awareness leads to overwhelm — celebrate that too.
It's the knowing itself that we celebrate.

THE SEVENTH RULE OF GRIEF CLUB:

Accept that there is nothing to FIX, and there is a lot to honour.

THE EIGHTH RULE OF GRIEF CLUB:

There are no rules for how to grieve,
just the option to build awareness and take action on repeat.

THE NINTH RULE OF GRIEF CLUB:

You get to make up any other rules you want:

INTRODUCTION

If you've been gifted this book or gifted it to yourself, I assume you are entering a phase of grief in your life. I make sure never to fully define grief, and over the next year I am sure that your own definition will be a living, breathing part of you that evolves as you do.

I personally define grief as ***the loss of anything meaningful*** (not only a physical death), ***and the human process and journey that follow it***. I only have one guide post when it comes to the journey — honour it — all of it.

You may have noticed I spell honour the Canadian way. That's intentional.

Although I've lived in the United States for most of my adult life, when it comes to this word, I truly believe that it's more of an "our" thing than an "or" thing.

Grief isn't something you fix; it's something you honour. There's no flash sale, weekend retreat or quickly found solution. We often dream of a comeback from grieving, when the healthiest thing we can do is aim to *come-through*, by waking up every day and honouring our relationship with loss and how we feel in each moment that follows.

Adapt the spelling of honour for yourself. It's an invitation to reframe the notion that your grief journey must inherently be lonely.

Remember that this is about you and your own grief process. Always use what works, and toss out what doesn't.

GRIEF IS THE MOST
NATURAL HUMAN
EXPERIENCE THERE IS,
AND YET SOMEHOW
THE MOST
UNCOMFORTABLE
AND UNPREDICTABLE.
LIKE ANY PROCESS,
WE MUST BE WILLING
TO EXPERIMENT AND
EVOLVE.

LIVING IN THE GRAY SPACE

Starting today, allow yourself to live in what cannot be defined, only experienced — Gray Space.

Here lives the known,
the unknown, the in-between,
the "I-don't-know-how-to-do-this" space,
the "I-feel-lost" space, the processing ...
the safe space.

Throughout this book you will find *actual* gray space. This is yours to write whatever you want to in the moment you come across that space or when the desire to add something lands for you.

The membership dues for Grief Club are in the unspoken commitment you make here to being curious and compassionate about a life in the gray space. There is no wrong or right, only your truth. Your truth neither defines you nor your grief; it's just plot points on a map that has an undecided destination. Doodle, scribble, write, journal, draw ... life after loss is messy, so your gray space can be too.

There are extra pages of gray space in the back of this book for when you need them.

HOW TO READ THIS BOOK

Let's do this together. To start, let's connect here daily for the next seven days. And then, let's spend a moment together once a week for the next year. I am your pocket pal now, I'm here when you need me.

I didn't study grief academically, I am just a guy who lost my brother to cancer, found my father after suicide, and lost my dear friend in an accident that left me re-learning to walk and make sense of the world. All of this happened in my 20s.

Navigating these complex grief processes lead me to develop the offerings you're reading here. And that's just what they are, unconditional offerings you can treat like experiments, that may or may not serve you in what can be an isolating and lonely journey forward.

Think of me as a grief "sibling". You may not always like me, want to face me, play with or hang out with me, but I'll always be your sibling and here for you when you come back. Even though I wrote this book, everything you do with it, will be about you. I'm just the Ron to your Harry—willing to go to ends of the earth with you but not in it to be the hero.

In a way we are all grieving a world we once knew. In a pandemic-possible world, our ways of grieving formally and informally have shifted. Our ability to gather to support each other has been threatened. Ceremonies and rites of passage our society has long-practiced have been minimized or passed over completely. *Real* life grief in a pandemic-possible world predates anything that's ever existed in the arena we now play in.

SPACE FOR NOTES ON YOUR DEFINITION OF GRIEF:

My brain tells me grief is …

My body says grief feels like …

My spirituality/ religion/ intuition says grief is …

With all this in mind,
I would define grief in one to two sentences today as …

" FOR WHAT IT'S WORTH: IT'S NEVER TOO LATE OR, IN MY CASE, TOO EARLY TO BE WHOEVER YOU WANT TO BE. THERE'S NO TIME LIMIT, STOP WHENEVER YOU WANT. YOU CAN CHANGE OR STAY THE SAME, THERE ARE NO RULES TO THIS THING. WE CAN MAKE THE BEST OR THE WORST OF IT. I HOPE YOU MAKE THE BEST OF IT. AND I HOPE YOU SEE THINGS THAT STARTLE YOU. I HOPE YOU FEEL THINGS YOU NEVER FELT BEFORE. I HOPE YOU MEET PEOPLE WITH A DIFFERENT POINT OF VIEW. I HOPE YOU LIVE A LIFE YOU'RE PROUD OF. IF YOU FIND THAT YOU'RE NOT, I HOPE YOU HAVE THE COURAGE TO START ALL OVER AGAIN. **"**

–Eric Roth, screenwriter, *The Curious Case of Benjamin Button*[i]

I'm not going to talk to you like you're a kid, and I won't pretend to be a doctor. I'm living in the grief arena too. If I had a choice I probably wouldn't be, but that's not how this works. I'm the one across the stadium covered in sweat and tears, that laughs whenever he can. (Yes, "Hi!") I'm just your peer. I'll talk to you like that friend who pops up upon request and shares manageable bites you can experiment with through your experience. What I can offer you is regular reminding that loss is normal, and I trust you to see that my humor is part of my own toolkit, because it has been central to honouring my own journey. I like to say "I'm equal parts "Find the funny" and "Honour the journey"."

Let me be that friend who gets the bill — seriously, I've been coached, therapy-ed and retreated. I've run a mental health company, explored my story by writing a memoir, and held workshops as a peer facilitator. I'm not the head of Grief Club; I'm a fellow traveler. I've experimented and explored the possibilities of my resilience and I want to share.

I'm passing down experiments that came to me from folks who invested in my survival. I include them because, when intertwined with my grief, they served me. If you want the story of how, you'll have to wait for my memoir. This book is about you, or at least an honest invitation for you to get to know yourself before, during and after a meaningful loss.

At times, in *Grief Club* I will quote someone that I think of as a "Grief Giant" or a person who has spent their life studying grief. As always, these offerings are meant to nourish you, for you to digest and then decide whether or not they serve you in the long run. They provide opportunities for discernment along the way. I stand on the shoulders of many but with you I will remain shoulder to shoulder. If something doesn't serve you, I'll be the first to open the window for you to throw it out and move on.

Above all else, this book isn't about discovering how messed up we are in the wake of loss, it's about gently and slowly discovering how truly resilient we are while honouring everything that makes us feel otherwise along the way.

While this book is structured and worded at some times for those experiencing the loss or death of another being, we can apply the experiments, ideas and offerings to the loss of anything meaningful to you. When a person being lost is referenced, just switch it out for what you are grieving.

This is (real life) Grief Club. A club that does not discriminate and eventually everyone will join.

Shall we get started?

Before you turn the page, close your eyes and take a deep breath.

I've told you my intentions, feel free to reflect on yours:

TEXT
GRIEF CLUB
TO
323-431-9241

my.community.com/griefclub

THE
SILENCE

DAY ONE

AFTER THE CASSEROLES AND CONDOLENCES
FADE AWAY THERE IS A SILENCE
THAT WILL BE WAITING FOR YOU ...
A SILENCE THAT MAY NEVER BE TRULY
SOOTHING BUT THAT IS SO NECESSARY —
IT IS THE SOUND EQUIVALENT
OF WHAT'S BEEN LOST ...

At first, it's hard to sit in that silence for longer than a few seconds. You want to turn the TV on, pick up your phone, call somebody, or literally run away. Trust that silence though ... sit in it a little longer each time, and honour everything you feel in your mind and body. Let the loss live, and if it gets too difficult, just know that I'll still be here when the silence comes, sending you love. This book will be here for you to open once a week, or as many times as you want for the next year. You can repeat, go back, jump forward or move slowly.

CONSCIOUS EMOTIONAL FITNESS CHECK-IN:

Choose one word in this moment to describe how you are feeling PHYSICALLY, MENTALLY AND EMOTIONALLY.

With AWARENESS of yourself in this moment how do you want to take ACTION?

OFFERING:

GET YOUR BEARINGS.

Treat the SILENT moments like a new friend.

Approach the few and fleeting moments of silence today with curiosity, compassion and kindness.

Notice how your body feels, what thoughts surface, what life in the midst of loss feels like right now.

Make notes of what comes up in silence – thoughts, feelings, what you want, wish or hope for. Let anything come up.

DAY TWO

IF NO ONE HAS MENTIONED THIS YET, LET ME BE THE FIRST TO SAY: YOU MAY BE IN SHOCK.

Because there is a perceived threat, your brain is in a survival state right now. A state where fear of the unknown prevails. You might be thinking, *this is the deepest loss I have ever felt — I won't forget any of this.*

And I would say, "Yes I thought so too."

I have been told I have a stenographer style memory. I can remember exactly what people say, when they say it and how. However, in the weeks after deaths and major life changes/ losses of relationships, opportunities or experiences that were meaningful to me, I seemed to lose that superpower completely. I wish someone had taken me aside in a warm way and said, "You may be in shock — and later you will have so many questions — let's leave a time capsule for when you're ready."

CONSCIOUS EMOTIONAL FITNESS CHECK-IN:

Choose one word in this moment to describe how you are feeling PHYSICALLY, MENTALLY AND EMOTIONALLY.

With AWARENESS of yourself in this moment how do you want to take ACTION?

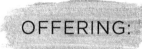
OFFERING:

RECORD TO REMEMBER.

With that in mind, today's offering is simple. As you navigate the next few hours, days, and weeks, make notes on your phone, take pictures, journal in the gray spaces here, or video. Whatever works for you. It may seem silly to record things now, but later you may be truly happy you did. And if not, you can always delete them.

Room to Notice and Record:

DAY THREE

Things get messy, muddled and well, I guess what I'm trying to say is, if today isn't really Day Three, don't worry about it. I'm here, within these pages, whenever you feel called to come back. The last thing I want is to add any shame or feelings of *fake* failure to your life. You can't fail at grief. You're safe. Speaking of safety, today's offering is about getting in touch with yourself, safely and honestly.

I want to introduce you to your lungs. If you haven't thought about them until now, that's okay, they've just been keeping you alive since you were born. Scientifically, they are part of our autonomic nervous system. What's that, you ask?

"The autonomic nervous system is a component of the peripheral nervous system that regulates involuntary physiologic processes including heart rate, blood pressure, respiration, digestion, and sexual arousal. It contains three anatomically distinct divisions: sympathetic, parasympathetic, and enteric."

Yes, I'm no pro, I just Googled it.[ii] Learning to become mindful of what's automatic and tapping into breath can be our most significant superpowers. This doesn't have to be full on meditation. I'm just saying that in moments of crisis, noticing my breath has been lifesaving.

CONSCIOUS EMOTIONAL FITNESS CHECK-IN:

Choose one word in this moment to describe how you are feeling PHYSICALLY, MENTALLY AND EMOTIONALLY.

With AWARENESS of yourself in this moment how do you want to take ACTION?

OFFERING:

BREATHE.

Now I'm just offering this ... if you Google (just like I did), you can actually type "breathwork when feeling _____" and you fill in the blank with how you're feeling. See what works. See what doesn't. But if you aren't already in tune with the superpower that is your breath, I'm telling you, you're going to want to hop on the bandwagon.

I like to breathe in through my nose for 5 seconds, hold for 5 seconds, breathe out for 5 seconds, and hold for 5 seconds. If you just tried that, congrats! You did a box breath. I do that until I feel grounded again. Sometimes seconds later and sometimes an hour later.

Feel free to do as many as you'd like now, or none at all.

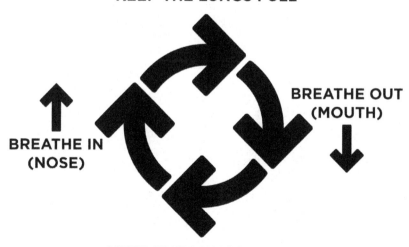

KEEP THE LUNGS FULL

BREATHE OUT (MOUTH)

BREATHE IN (NOSE)

KEEP THE LUNGS EMPTY

DAY FOUR

How are you doing?

How are you feeling?

I'm sorry for your loss.

My deepest condolences.

What are you going to do now?

Are you sure you're okay?!

Pause. Let's remember that day three offering. Yes, you got it. Deep Breath.

If I could re-train everyone around you right now, I would tell them to stick with one phrase: *What does support look like for you right now?* and allow *you* to respond to them honestly.

And "I don't know" is a perfectly great answer, by the way.

We can't change what other people say or do. We *can* teach people how to treat us around our loss. I wish I'd known this a lot earlier.

CONSCIOUS EMOTIONAL FITNESS CHECK-IN:

Choose one word in this moment to describe how you are feeling PHYSICALLY, MENTALLY AND EMOTIONALLY.

With AWARENESS of yourself in this moment how do you want to take ACTION?

OFFERING:

RESILIENCE RESPONSES.

Just a friendly reminder that you can **NOT** control anyone else around you. It takes up valuable energy, time and resources you need to even try or think about trying to change others, not to mention the spent energy you'd use to even complain about how you *wish* you could change others.

The offering is <u>to stop trying.</u>

Some Resilience Reponses and Reframes:

How are you doing? How are you feeling?

"Right now, I'm just focusing on be-ing, and trying to honour what comes up, thank you."

I'm sorry for your loss.

"Thank you, your support means a lot to me right now. I think what I am looking for at this moment is …"

My deepest condolences. It will get better.

"I appreciate you showing up for me right now. I'm going to honour how I feel before jumping to silver linings."

What are you going to do now?

"My intention is to healthily honour everything I'm feeling right now while taking slow steps forward in my healing journey."

Are you sure you're okay?!

If they say this, just hit them. (Joking). **Maybe something like:**

"I'm feeling so many things right now, but if I can figure out what I need in terms of support I will reach out."

These are just my offerings. You get the gist though. Write down a few of your own responses. A "Resilience Response" has one main quality – it energizes you when you use it. Remember, energy is precious right now and this is your loss and your healing journey.

Room for some reframes of your own:

ONCE YOU ENTER GRIEF CLUB,
YOU NEVER GET OUT. THAT'S THE TRUTH WE
MISS WITH SYMPATHY CARDS AND FLOWERS
THAT DIE JUST LIKE THOSE WE LOST.
BUT IN REAL LIFE GRIEF, THERE IS A RADIATING
RESILIENCE TO BE DISCOVERED —
IT'S JUST FACTUALLY TRUE.
WE HAVE ALL LOST WHAT'S MEANINGFUL
AND WE ARE STILL HERE.

DAY FIVE

You might have heard some people refer to the five or six stages of grief. I didn't bring this up earlier because I wanted you to experientially learn, (yes in just five days), that although these stages exist, they don't always happen in order and can also overlap and get messy.

Stage 1 – Denial

Stage 2 – Anger

Stage 3 – Bargaining

Stage 4 – Depression

Stage 5 – Acceptance[iii]

Stage 6 – Meaning[iv]

I don't know about you, but in the hours and days after a loss I bounced back and forth between all of these. Especially the first three; with no clear boundaries or ability to make sense around where I found myself and when. The stages can be a circle, a cyclone, or a cornucopia of confusing crap. (Yeah, I said it.)

CONSCIOUS EMOTIONAL FITNESS CHECK-IN:

Choose one word in this moment to describe how you are feeling PHYSICALLY, MENTALLY AND EMOTIONALLY.

With AWARENESS of yourself in this moment how do you want to take ACTION?

OFFERING:

SWIRL.

Accept that this isn't going to make sense now. Accept that there can be a **SWIRL** of these feelings and stages. And if you don't want to accept that — well, the first stage is called denial for a reason. Remember to **"honour the journey"**. Whisper that to yourself whenever your grief feels unnatural, debilitating, or shameful. This will stop your negative thought patterns from becoming a habit you can't easily break away from. No idea what that means? Don't worry, you can thank me later. Just interrupt thoughts that don't serve you even if you have to say "CANCEL" out loud.

WHAT'S A LIMITING BELIEF?

> **"**LIMITING BELIEFS AND "SHOULDS" ARE EXACTLY WHAT THEIR ACRONYM IS: BS. SUPPOSED TO'S, HAVE TO'S, NEED TO'S, AND SHOULDS ARE ALL ONE-OPTION LIMITING BELIEFS ACCORDING TO YOUR BUY-IN OF SOMEONE ELSE'S SKEWED VIEWS OF THE WORLD. YOU FIND YOUR TRUTH WHEN IT FEELS LIKE CHOICE.**"**

–Jenifer Merifield, Extraordinary Life Podcast

DAY SIX

Hey! I just want to start today by saying: You're a Badass! Just for showing up, again. You've probably realized that it seems like it would be easier to just ignore all of this than "honour it". While it may seem like it would feel good now, I'd be a terrible grief sibling if I didn't also tell you that ignoring the pain *now* will create a lot of personal and even financial costs later.

Keep honouring, keep breathing, keep accepting what shows up. Just trust me, like I trust you. After tomorrow, we will just check in once a week so you can be in the arena with your grief experiments and apply them to your life and develop your own toolbox, one that works for you.

CONSCIOUS EMOTIONAL FITNESS CHECK-IN:

Choose one word in this moment to describe how you are feeling PHYSICALLY, MENTALLY AND EMOTIONALLY.

With AWARENESS of yourself in this moment how do you want to take ACTION?

OFFERING:

REST.

Yup, that's it.

You've had a major loss. Don't learn anything today. Just rest.

I realize that if you've lost a special person, you may be overwhelmed with planning how to honour them in a special way in the coming time. I still have to be the friend that says, rest, even for ten minutes at a time. Take deep breaths. Use those lungs.

Also, ask for help and actually accept it.

There is no wrong way to honour someone.

> **GRIEF IS VISCERAL, NOT REASONABLE: THE HOWLING AT THE CENTER OF GRIEF IS RAW AND REAL. IT IS LOVE IN ITS MOST WILD FORM.**

– Megan Devine[v]

DAY SEVEN

This may all seem very real and completely dream-like at the same time. My doctors and coaches have told me that sometimes we disconnect as a defense mechanism, and I know that at other times we feel so deeply we would do anything to make it stop. There's room for all of it.

A gentle reminder from Dr. Michael Gervais that may be helpful to remember along the way:

"The larger the space between who a person SAYS they are and who they ACTUALLY are, the more pain that person feels when it's exposed. Be aligned. Be you."[vi]

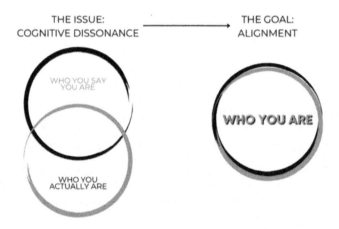

THE ISSUE:
COGNITIVE DISSONANCE

THE GOAL:
ALIGNMENT

WHO YOU SAY YOU ARE

WHO YOU ARE

WHO YOU ACTUALLY ARE

CONSCIOUS EMOTIONAL FITNESS CHECK-IN:

Choose one word in this moment to describe how you are feeling PHYSICALLY, MENTALLY AND EMOTIONALLY.

With AWARENESS of yourself in this moment how do you want to take ACTION?

OFFERING:

Today's offering is to carve out some time to explain this loss to yourself. You may be thinking, *I don't need to explain this to myself, I'm living in the loss, thank you.* I get that, but there's a deeper part of you that needs to hear from you. The part of you that thought this would never happen, could never happen ... the child within you.

Here's the experiment, hell, it's so important that just this once I'm going to call it a *challenge*: Write a letter to a child you know or to your younger self as a child. One that would be understanding of your specific type of loss for the first time ever. The reader would be taking a break from learning to read and write to hear this, so please be gentle, honest and above all else help them to fully understand what you're experiencing and what loss feels like. After you finish writing it, read it out loud, or even record it on your phone and listen back. Notice what you notice and feel what you feel.

You're going to want to skip this one. But I promise if you do it, I won't bother you again for a whole week. Deal? Let me get you started:

" DEAR CHILD... "

THE
SWIRL

WEEK 2

I'm glad that you have come back to this. Have you been feeling stuck?

Part of honouring the journey is honouring the stuck-ness. There's no easy fix, although I'm sure you've realized now that deep breathing during those moments can be very grounding.

What happens next is specific to your journey.

When my brother died, I launched into overachieving and do-ing. When my father passed, I sat on my hands and counted and only slept for a few hours in the daylight; I was afraid of the dark, of everything really. When my friend passed, I was hospitalized and didn't get to be a part of any of her memorial services. I was just numb, heartbroken and unsure I would be able to move forward with this grief. There was no right answer, only what is, in the moment.

CONSCIOUS EMOTIONAL FITNESS CHECK-IN:

Choose one word in this moment to describe how you are feeling PHYSICALLY, MENTALLY AND EMOTIONALLY.

With AWARENESS of yourself in this moment how do you want to take ACTION?

OFFERING:

MOVE.

Experiment with a movement schedule. It can be as simple as standing up once every hour with the help of reminders on your phone or computer, or as intense as heading to fitness classes every morning for the next week. The commitment is to move. Move daily and hourly. Shift energy by stretching or walking. Just move.

Keep a movement journal this week in the notes on your phone or even text me every time you move. Without putting too much thought into the why or the how, just move as much as possible. Get out of your head and into your body.

As Nora McInerny so eloquently said in her viral TED talk about grief:

" WE DON'T "MOVE ON" FROM GRIEF.
WE MOVE FORWARD WITH IT.[vii] "

WEEK 3

What's one thing you do every day? As a child the answer might not have been to brush my teeth, but as an adult who fears dental bills and just appreciates hygiene I would say "brushing my teeth."

Make a list of things you do EVERY DAY:

(It can be beyond simple and obvious — like waking up, putting your glasses on, your feet touching the floor for the first time, or something we all know happens, but we may not think about, like flushing the toilet.)

CONSCIOUS EMOTIONAL FITNESS CHECK-IN:

Choose one word in this moment to describe how you are feeling PHYSICALLY, MENTALLY AND EMOTIONALLY.

With AWARENESS of yourself in this moment how do you want to take ACTION?

OFFERING:

PICK ONE THING THAT HAPPENS EVERY DAY.

Once you have that thing, what's one thing you could say out loud or in your head every day that would really serve you right now. If you had me to remind you of one thing right now, What do you want to hear?

I'm safe.

I am resilient.

I am capable of honouring my journey.

Loss is a beautiful part of life.

Follow this, you !@%#!

No judgement, it's what you **WANT** to hear right now.

Mine is: "I am aligned with my own personal frequency of optimal health, wealth and my divine right to be loved and love unconditionally." And I do it every time I brush my teeth.

This is an experiment, not a cure, just try it for a week.

Say out loud to yourself what you want to hear, every time you do_____ in a day.

Stuck on what to say? Feel silly? Good. You're normal. Set a timer on your phone for three minutes and just write anything that comes to mind. Read through them and whatever feels the best — just go with it.

When I

(pick daily activity)

I will say

my.community.com/griefclub

WEEK 4

It's been a calendar "month" now. How does that feel? Like it's been longer? Shorter? Like you should be farther ahead, feeling better, or back to full speed?

Let's Pause. If you're nodding, you have been measuring your grief.

YOU CAN'T BE SMARTER THAN GRIEF;

YOU CAN ONLY BE SMART ENOUGH

TO HONOUR IT.

Measuring can sound like:

"I should be feeling better by now" or "I can't believe how much I have cried" or "I only cried one time". It is in comments like "I get angry a lot more than I should now", "I thought after a month I would be able to do more" and "I've only gone to the cemetery twice."

CONSCIOUS EMOTIONAL FITNESS CHECK-IN:

Choose one word in this moment to describe how you are feeling PHYSICALLY, MENTALLY AND EMOTIONALLY.

With AWARENESS of yourself in this moment how do you want to take ACTION?

OFFERING:

STOP MEASURING YOUR GRIEF.

This week's offering, like all offerings, is an experiment. What happens if every time you find yourself measuring your grief, you stop everything you're doing or saying, smile and forgive yourself? Then switch over to noticing what's happening in the moment when you find yourself measuring. Are you doing it in the presence of others? Alone? With those whom share the loss?

As my coach Jenifer Merifield used to say:

"According to whom or compared to what?"

Keep notes or just notice what you notice. How does it feel to stop measuring around your loss and grief journey? If it feels good, maybe we put the "noticing tool" in the toolbox. As always, it's up to you.

WHAT YOU FOCUS ON EXPANDS.

I wrote this at the beach one day when I was feeling overwhelmed by my grief journey.

"As the sun set, I felt a sadness that seemed to stem from the place I sense my soul has been hiding. I was frozen by the idea of darkness. I grieved the sun's light like I grieved my brother and father. I put my hand on my heart as Jen had taught me and whispered, "Let joy guide you", took a deep breath and turned around. In all that worry I hadn't realized a full moon had illuminated behind me. There I was, and not alone in the dark for even a second, except for when I chose to blink. But I didn't blink — I was lost and found all in a moment; just a boy again mesmerized by the beauty of the moon."

CONSCIOUS EMOTIONAL FITNESS CHECK-IN:

Choose one word in this moment to describe how you are feeling PHYSICALLY, MENTALLY AND EMOTIONALLY.

With AWARENESS of yourself in this moment how do you want to take ACTION?

OFFERING:

NOTICE.

Experiment with noticing what you find yourself focusing on (sometimes obsessively so) and get active in asking: Do I want this thought to expand? Also, if this thought became actionable for my well-being how would it sound?

"*I will never be okay*" versus "*I want help with …*"

Saying things like "I will never be okay" prepares your brain to make a list of evidence for why that statement is true.

"I want help with …" can turn into an honest and constructive list of what will help you honour the journey and be ACTIVE in it.

WEEK 6

Do we want to take the breathing to the next level? There can be a lot of moments of tension, force and downright stress when coming to grips with the reality of any loss. It seems over simplified, but bringing back the reminder around your lungs, the ability to breathe and its power to gain presence and calm down your nervous system, is a life raft that's always there for you.

" IT TURNS OUT THAT WHEN BREATHING AT A NORMAL RATE, OUR LUNGS WILL ABSORB ONLY ABOUT A QUARTER OF THE AVAILABLE OXYGEN IN THE AIR. THE MAJORITY OF THAT OXYGEN IS EXHALED BACK OUT. BY TAKING LONGER BREATHS, WE ALLOW OUR LUNGS TO SOAK UP MORE IN FEWER BREATHS. **"**

– James Nestor[viii]

CONSCIOUS EMOTIONAL FITNESS CHECK-IN:

Choose one word in this moment to describe how you are feeling PHYSICALLY, MENTALLY AND EMOTIONALLY.

With AWARENESS of yourself in this moment how do you want to take ACTION?

OFFERING:

BREATHE.

Search different breathing techniques and breathwork class options. Pick one way to expand your knowledge of breathing. Do two to three breath experiments this week based on what you find.

Examples of Breath Experiments:

- Breathe only through your nose during certain activities or timed periods
- Do box breaths between Zoom calls or meetings
- Try the 4-7-8 breathing technique for five minutes when you feel something triggering

DEEPER DIVE

Read *Breath: The New Science of Lost* Art by James Nestor

Google and YouTube are free. Which means you're rich!

(Suggestions: Wim Hof, nose breathing, morning breathing, breathing exercises for sleep, heart brain coherence breathing)

WEEK 7

YOUR GRATITUDE IS YOUR GRIEF,
AND YOUR GRIEF CAN BE FULL OF GRATITUDE.

It can feel wild or inappropriate to consider gratitude when you are grieving, but in retrospect, I wish I started the practice of consciously acknowledging what I appreciate and am grateful for much sooner.

If it feels too early, too annoying, or too anything to even think about gratitude at this moment, that is totally your call. Fold the top right corner of this page and know that when you're ready you'll come back to it.

CONSCIOUS EMOTIONAL FITNESS CHECK-IN:

Choose one word in this moment to describe how you are feeling PHYSICALLY, MENTALLY AND EMOTIONALLY.

With AWARENESS of yourself in this moment how do you want to take ACTION?

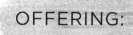
OFFERING:

GRATE-FUEL.

Start simple.

Every day this week, at a set time, share three things you are grateful for. You can journal it, put it in your notes, tweet it, or even invite a friend to receive yours and share theirs as well.

Think of yourself as having an empty fuel tank each day – luckily, the cost of gas is cheap. Just three things that you are grateful for.

HINT: Feeling stuck on this gratitude thing? Tune into your five senses – what do you appreciate in this present moment?

Text me your three each day.

WEEK 8

Linear time would say that has been two months of you honouring this journey. Grief can feel like it has its own timeline though and that's the one we honour. What's important is not measuring time and any sort of results but noticing what is and isn't working for you in honouring and showing up fully in your grief.

CONSCIOUS EMOTIONAL FITNESS CHECK-IN:

Choose one word in this moment to describe how you are feeling PHYSICALLY, MENTALLY AND EMOTIONALLY.

With AWARENESS of yourself in this moment how do you want to take ACTION?

OFFERING:

CHECK IN.

Take this list of all the things we have covered so far. For each, answer yes or no.

Then ask yourself, would I like to keep this tool?

- Am I checking in daily with how I feel emotionally, mentally and physically?
- Am I allowing silence?
- Am I recording memories and experiences related to grief?
- Am I breathing?
- Am I trying to control other people?
- Am I accepting my swirl of grief stages and emotions?
- Am I resting?
- Am I speaking and nurturing myself like a child in difficult moments?
- Am I moving?
- Am I affirming and keeping it anchored to a daily activity?
- Am I measuring or noticing?
- Am I changing my focus before it expands?
- Am I using breath to change my state? Fall asleep? Or calm down?
- Am I allowing gratitude to be a part of my grief journey?

Shelley Paxton:
What does that mean for you and what has that grief process and journey of moving through it looked like?

Addison:

Now, honouring the journey. When I say that,
what I tend to mean is actually accepting and
working through whatever comes up, not what we've
designed to come up, or hope to come up, or plan
to come up, or work to perfect coming up. But what
actually does.

Rebel Souls Podcast: A Masterclass in Grief and Emotional Fitness

WEEK 9

Comparing and competition are not friends to us Grief Club siblings. Chances are you shared this loss with at least one other person or that the loss affects others around you. When we give energy to comparing our loss with others or even comparing them to our own past losses we are consuming energy that could be used for optimal healing and conscious thought.

Take a moment to consider how being competitive with or comparing your grief has really served you?

Sometimes we don't realize we are doing it. Thinking about it even when you say or think things like, "This hurts but at least it wasn't _____."

Does that help honour what you're feeling? Let's find out.

CONSCIOUS EMOTIONAL FITNESS CHECK-IN:

Choose one word in this moment to describe how you are feeling PHYSICALLY, MENTALLY AND EMOTIONALLY.

With AWARENESS of yourself in this moment how do you want to take ACTION?

 OFFERING:

NO COMPARING.

Yes, that's the experiment. One week with no comparing, no competition, no one-upping ... nada. See how it feels and change your life accordingly. If it doesn't benefit you in anyway, why keep it? Have fun and be gentle with catching yourself. Just so we are clear, that's none of the following:

verb

gerund or present participle: **comparing**

> **estimate, measure, or note the similarity or dissimilarity between.**

Of course, this is an experiment to see how not comparing can really serve you in honouring your grief journey. So, if you do catch yourself, lovingly bring your attention back to the intentions of all of our experiments: curiosity, self-compassion and kindness.

WEEK 10

The A word growing up was something we were taught not say. The A word in grief makes us afraid we might be called that other A word.

Anger is defined as a strong feeling of annoyance, displeasure, or hostility in the dictionary, but as always, feel free to create your own definition that resonates for you. Loss is annoying. Loss is not pleasurable. Loss can bring out parts of us that want to fight to feel normal again and that may seem hostile. Anger is part of grief, and you are allowed to be angry. Period.

As Brene Brown says in her most recent book *Atlas of the Heart*, "Anger is an action emotion- we want to do something when we feel it and when were on the receiving end of it."

I also loved how natural this quote from a recent NPR article made me feel:

"Grief is like someone turned up the volume dial all of a sudden. The emotion that I think often interferes with our relationships and friendships when we're grieving is anger, because the anger feels so intense."[x]

CONSCIOUS EMOTIONAL FITNESS CHECK-IN:

Choose one word in this moment to describe how you are feeling PHYSICALLY, MENTALLY AND EMOTIONALLY.

With AWARENESS of yourself in this moment how do you want to take ACTION?

OFFERING:

BE ANGRY.

Google healthy ways to let out anger. Pick one. Try it. Don't think too much. There are actually places now that you can go and pay to break things in a room or throw axes at a target. This can be fun and therapeutic. The takeaway is that there are no good or bad emotions, just constructive and deconstructive ones.

Let's just allow ANGER this week. The goal of this experiment is to relieve yourself of any judgement and process how you really feel. There is no way to fail, only ways to learn more.

For a **DEEPER DIVE** into anger and other emotions: Read *Atlas of the Heart: Mapping Meaningful Connection and The Language of Human Experience* by Brene Brown.[ix]

WEEK 11

Hopefully, you got curious and stayed compassionate enough to allow anger as a healthy emotion last week. How did it feel? Think it might serve you to allow more emotions as they come up? Good, we agree. Now let's take a look at the image below and really just digest how much further we can go when describing how we are feeling.[xi]

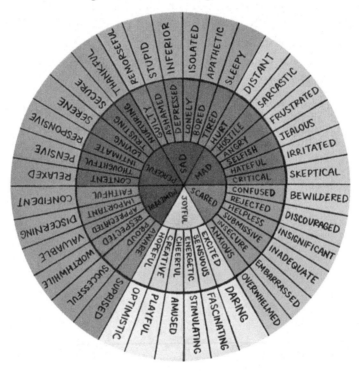

CONSCIOUS EMOTIONAL FITNESS CHECK-IN:

Choose one word in this moment to describe how you are feeling PHYSICALLY, MENTALLY AND EMOTIONALLY.

With AWARENESS of yourself in this moment how do you want to take ACTION?

OFFERING:

FEEL IT ALL.

Take a look at the image on the last page. In your spare time this week …
and before you say "I don't have spare time" … let's just say this experiment
in grief is a priority. You will find the time because you are a badass creator.
Sorry, but grief siblings don't let other grief siblings fall to the side of the
arena. Rest and avoidance are different.

Now back to the experiment, start at one of the main emotions, like
MAD, and then start to reflect on how all the different sub emotions feel
for you. What is your personal difference between frustrated and hateful?
Or between distant and irritated? Just explore and notice what comes up.

Hint: When you feel a certain emotion, what is the experience of that
through your senses, body and overall energy levels?

This week, when doing daily emotional fitness check-ins with yourself,
start to get really specific about what you are feeling and where you feel it
in your body.

WEEK 12

Three months - have you been doing daily emotional fitness check-ins? What grief experiments have led to getting to know yourself a little better? No wrong answers ... this is a check in.

Are you breathing? No? Want to start again? Before going to the next page, take a moment to reflect on what has made the greatest difference for you in the last three months.

What do you want more of?

I'm leaving you some room to write, scribble, make notes, claw your nails into the page. Have at it:

CONSCIOUS EMOTIONAL FITNESS CHECK-IN:

Choose one word in this moment to describe how you are feeling PHYSICALLY, MENTALLY AND EMOTIONALLY.

With AWARENESS of yourself in this moment how do you want to take ACTION?

OFFERING:

CHECK IN.

You've built awareness around your grief and loss, now let's get active in realizing what ACTION feels like in relation to that awareness. We won't do this every month. I just really wanted to remind you of the learnings while everything you're feeling is still so new.

- Am I checking in daily with how I feel emotionally, mentally and physically?
- Am I allowing silence?
- Am I recording memories and experiences related to my grief?
- Am I breathing?
- Am I trying to control other people?
- Am I accepting my swirl of grief stages and emotions?
- Am I resting?
- Am I speaking and nurturing myself like a child in difficult moments?
- Am I moving?
- Am I affirming anchored with a daily activity?
- Am I measuring or noticing?
- Am I changing my focus before it expands?
- Am I using breath to change my state? Fall asleep? Or calm down?
- Am I allowing gratitude to be a part of my grief journey?
- Am I comparing/competing?
- Am I expressing my anger and other emotions healthily?
- Am I allowing my emotions without judgements/getting curious about how they feel ?

WEEK 13

What keeps you awake at night? What are you so passionate (notice I didn't say stressed) about that it gets your whole being energized to change, solve or focus on a purpose? What can you just *not* think about? What gets to you? You know the thing.

I find myself raging about how the mental health system works in America, or how hard it is to adopt children that have no homes, and also more casually about how stupid certain roads were built and how I would have designed Los Angeles differently.

Let's talk about RAGE. It can actually be helpful, if we stop hiding from it. When attending a talk at Modern Elder Academy in Baja this year lead by Kay Scorah, I learned that rage creates focus, which creates purpose. So, *do not go gentle* into that grieving night … rage rage, my friend, against the dying of the light.

CONSCIOUS EMOTIONAL FITNESS CHECK-IN:

Choose one word in this moment to describe how you are feeling PHYSICALLY, MENTALLY AND EMOTIONALLY.

With AWARENESS of yourself in this moment how do you want to take ACTION?

RAGE!

Set aside time by yourself, with a safe friend or mental health professional to be honest about what makes you RAGE in this moment. Nothing is too big or too small. As we know, measuring doesn't serve us very well when it comes to our emotions but allowing them does. Get feisty with a pen or choose to yell it out. What can you *not* stand to hold inside for another minute? Anything boiling just beneath the surface? You got this. Set a timer for how long you'll vent these feelings and then plan for a grounding exercise after. Here's some literary go-go juice:

DO NOT GO GENTLE INTO THAT GOOD NIGHT

Do not go gentle into that good night,
Old age should burn and rave at close of day;
Rage, rage against the dying of the light.

Though wise men at their end know dark is right,
Because their words had forked no lightning they
Do not go gentle into that good night.

Good men, the last wave by, crying how bright
Their frail deeds might have danced in a green bay,
Rage, rage against the dying of the light.

Wild men who caught and sang the sun in flight,
And learn, too late, they grieved it on its way,
Do not go gentle into that good night.

Grave men, near death, who see with blinding sight
Blind eyes could blaze like meteors and be gay,
Rage, rage against the dying of the light.

And you, my father, there on the sad height,
Curse, bless, me now with your fierce tears, I pray.
Do not go gentle into that good night.
Rage, rage against the dying of the light.

– Dylan Thomas[x]

THE
SURVIVOR

WEEK 14

Trying to make deals is normal.

Are you a good negotiator? Do you like a good bargain? Have you found yourself wanting to make deals with a force greater than you or those directly involved in what/who you are grieving? Yeah, that happens, in fact it happens so much that our friend Dr. Kubler-Ross suggested a whole stage of grief called Bargaining.

"BARGAINING TAKES PLACE WITHIN THE MIND BY TRYING TO EXPLAIN THE THINGS THAT COULD HAVE DONE DIFFERENTLY OR BETTER. "IF ONLY WE HAD GOTTEN A SECOND OPINION."
"IF ONLY WE COULD HAVE TAKEN HER TO THE HOSPITAL SOONER." "IF ONLY I HAD TREATED AUNT NANCY BETTER." THE BARGAIN STRUCK IS NOT ONE THAT COULD ACTUALLY BE KEPT, BUT IT ASSISTS IN BRINGING MORE CONTROL BY IDENTIFYING WHAT COULD HAVE - OR SHOULD HAVE - BEEN DONE TO HANDLE THE CIRCUMSTANCE MORE EFFECTIVELY."[xii]

CONSCIOUS EMOTIONAL FITNESS CHECK-IN:

Choose one word in this moment to describe how you are feeling PHYSICALLY, MENTALLY AND EMOTIONALLY.

With AWARENESS of yourself in this moment how do you want to take ACTION?

OFFERING:

BEG, BARGAIN, BE.

As an experiment this week, verbally or in writing, say out loud or put to paper those wild bargains you would like to make with yourself, with your greater force, with your family, your job, your past loves. No rules here. If you have already found yourself trying to make deals – record the ones you remember with love.

A little peer perspective for this one, (take it or leave it). When I lost my brother to brain cancer, I had many nights screaming at my greater force begging them to bring my brother back and put me in the ground. Even if I never knew the difference. When I lost my dad and my dear friend, I tried to skip what felt like the silliness of the bargaining stage. I'm not going to beg for something that can't happen I thought, but eventually the human part of my soul had to at least try. I needed to know without a doubt I did everything I could for it to not be true before accepting it in any way. To make the deal to get them back, to make deals that someone would show up and love me through this ... constantly working out what I would be willing to give to make reality go away.

Much like the genie's rules in "Aladdin", the bargains made in grief have limitations: We can't bring people back from the dead, we can't make anyone fall in love with us and ... we can't wish for more wishes. But we wouldn't be human beings if we didn't try. So have at it. Be an excellent grief negotiator. What bargaining do you have in you?

WEEK 15

Over the past while we have been experimenting in anger, rage, focus and you may be coming down from a week of intense bargaining. If you're anything like me, the silence, the swirl, the shame and the survivor in you, may all be what's keeping you up at night?

I personally fall asleep every night to Matthew McConaughey's sleep story on Calm, along with ear plugs and an eye mask. These are all things I never did before I was in Grief Club.

Words from two Sleep Giants:

CONSCIOUS EMOTIONAL FITNESS CHECK-IN:

Choose one word in this moment to describe how you are feeling PHYSICALLY, MENTALLY AND EMOTIONALLY.

With AWARENESS of yourself in this moment how do you want to take ACTION?

" ONE OF THE LEAST DISCUSSED BENEFITS (OR
MIRACLES, REALLY) OF SLEEP: THE WAY IT ALLOWS
US, ONCE WE RETURN FROM OUR NIGHT'S JOURNEY,
TO SEE THE WORLD ANEW, WITH FRESH EYES AND
A REINVIGORATED SPIRIT, TO STEP OUT OF TIME
AND COME BACK TO OUR LIVES RESTORED. **"**

–Arianna Huffington, *The Sleep Revolution:
Transforming Your Life, One Night at a Time*[xiii]

" WHEN IT COMES TO GETTING A GOOD NIGHT'S
SLEEP, YOU SHOULDN'T HAVE TO JUMP THROUGH A
BUNCH OF HOOPS TO GET THE REJUVENATING REST
YOU NEED. SOMETIMES THE DIFFERENCE BETWEEN
POOR SLEEP AND RESTFUL SLEEP REALLY IS JUST A
FEW HEALTHY LIFESTYLE CHANGES. **"**

–Michael J. Breus, PhD[xiv]

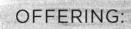

OFFERING:

SLEEP = RADICAL RECOVERY.

This week, pay attention to your sleep habits. Notice what's changed about your sleep during the grief journey, including right before bed and upon waking. On nights where you do get rest, what's different about your surroundings and routine versus the nights where you don't get rest? Make a sleep journal, track it on a wearable electronic app or device but let's start to realize the value of rest on a more scientific level. Get on Google, find some podcasts with sleep experts, learn everything you can about your own sleep habits this week.

Sleeping like a baby? Amazing! Do some noticing around your process so you can lock it in and be aware of how it differs from one night to the next. But mostly enjoy and maybe even build some around gratitude getting rest.

Considering the scientific benefits of proper sleep – this may be an experiment that makes you want to invest more. Maybe read Ariana Huffington's book or give The Sleep Doctor a call.

WEEK 16

Do you have the energy to resume life and deal with all that love with nowhere to go? How are you fueling yourself to deal with all you are dealing with? Never thought about it? That's okay too.

During my grief processes I barely ate in the first few months. My mind became cloudy, and I was easily agitated. I attributed it to the grieving and never stopped to notice that I wasn't eating enough to keep a person of my size and weight alive, never mind in a vital state to face all I was struggling with. When I did eat, I was eating very inflammatory foods which I later learned were contributing to a lot of the extra physical pain I was feeling.

If my dear friend and nutrition coach Jared Tavolosien hadn't gently offered to help me navigate my food choices and get curious about how my body worked, I would never have thought to pay attention to something so obvious.

We are what we eat.

CONSCIOUS EMOTIONAL FITNESS CHECK-IN:

Choose one word in this moment to describe how you are feeling PHYSICALLY, MENTALLY AND EMOTIONALLY.

With AWARENESS of yourself in this moment how do you want to take ACTION?

OFFERING:

NURTURE.

Last week we got focused on noticing our sleep and rest routine. Let's do the same this week around how we are fueling ourselves with food and hydration. Without judgement, this week's experiment is just about noticing what you are eating and when. Awareness comes before any sort of action.

Create a Food/Hydration Journal

Include what you're consuming, how much and the times you ate at, and how you felt 20 minutes after doing so. Just a few words. Remember to use feelings, not thoughts.

This experiment is all about noticing what choices energize us and which ones make it more difficult to deal with being in Grief Club.

Have fun with this, notice the word diet is not in the experiment offering.

WEEK 17

When we lose someone and we are mourning, we sometimes can't see that we have started to build a new relationship with them. It is in a new form, but a relationship with their memory, their legacy, their belongings, or their teachings is still very much alive as we move forward with our grief.

How is your *new* relationship with who or what's been lost coming along?

Take a moment, a few deep breaths and have an honest dialogue with yourself.

It might feel like the time to talk about your loss and remember them. You may feel that people who were affected by this loss or supporting you have moved on. I'm here with you and I want to hear about who you're honouring in this grief process.

CONSCIOUS EMOTIONAL FITNESS CHECK-IN:

Choose one word in this moment to describe how you are feeling PHYSICALLY, MENTALLY AND EMOTIONALLY.

With AWARENESS of yourself in this moment how do you want to take ACTION?

GET LOST IN MUSIC.

Let's pick one song that reminds you of them or the time in your life you're missing. Listen to it daily this week. If you can, listen once in the morning and once in the evening. See how it feels different each time and what feelings or sensations come up for you. Journal or talk to a grief sibling about it.

Email it to me: share@mygriefclub.com

I mean it. Let's honour them together.

We will add it to the Grief Club Spotify list, and you'll know it's your song.

WEEK 18

Sometimes grief can come with a lot of peer help: support from friends, family and community. It is important to keep in mind that this type of support is lifesaving and absolutely necessary. Sometimes we also want to invest in professional help when it comes to aligning our mental health and grief journeys.

If you broke your arm and had exposed bone and damaged nerves right now, there are things you would allow a friend to do like stick with you before, during and after getting the immediate professional/medical help you need or want. The same applies to your grief journey. Boundaries around who and how we let our grief community support us are essential to our emotional well-being and fitness.

CONSCIOUS EMOTIONAL FITNESS CHECK-IN:

Choose one word in this moment to describe how you are feeling PHYSICALLY, MENTALLY AND EMOTIONALLY.

With AWARENESS of yourself in this moment how do you want to take ACTION?

ASSESS.

Do a mental health check-in/ screening with a professional or through a professional resource. You don't have to do anything with the information you gather. You may be inspired to hire a coach, therapist or see a doctor. You may find you are right where you are meant to be. Make a list of trusted peers vs. professionals.

As always, don't think of this as a self-diagnosis tool but rather as an experiment and more than that, an investment in building a team around you for if and when you feel that you might need more help than a peer can provide.

Peers   Professionals

WEEK 19

I'll go first:

July 21st, September 1st, March 14th. Fresh flowers. New car smell. The taste of metal in my mouth. Headlights. Extension cords. Driving in the rain. Suicide scenes on TV film. Gaslighting. Sirens. Hospitals. Songs. Weather changes. Pain points in my body ... I could go on.

The list above will most likely mean nothing to you, but to me, these dates, times, experiences, and sensations are part of my daily walk through an emotional minefield.

I wrote an article on triggers here:

https://weareneveralone.co/blog/addison-brasil/

CONSCIOUS EMOTIONAL FITNESS CHECK-IN:

Choose one word in this moment to describe how you are feeling PHYSICALLY, MENTALLY AND EMOTIONALLY.

With AWARENESS of yourself in this moment how do you want to take ACTION?

OFFERING:

TRIGGER WARNING.

Make a list of what/who/where/when you experience triggers. This is private. Are there items on this list for example, like fresh flowers or a specific place, that you'd like to set the intention of beginning to change your relationship with so that you can experience it again without feeling so triggered in your grief process?

Remember to set yourself up with a self-care hour after doing this deeper experiment. Talk about it with your peers and your pros. At the very least doing this experiment allows us to let some close people in on what the triggers are, so they can help us healthily approach them. Because of my own transparency with triggers and openness about this process, I will get loving texts that say, "Be careful watching Season 2 Episode 6 of this show" – and I know someone that cares about me understands something in that episode will be a painful trigger for me.

Some spoiler alerts are the best way not to spoil your grief resilience journey.

> **"** IN ORDER TO CHANGE, PEOPLE NEED TO BECOME AWARE OF THEIR SENSATIONS AND THE WAY THAT THEIR BODIES INTERACT WITH THE WORLD AROUND THEM. PHYSICAL SELF-AWARENESS IS THE FIRST STEP IN RELEASING THE TYRANNY OF THE PAST. **"**
>
> –Bessel A. van der Kolk[xv]

WEEK 20

Now that we know each other a little better. I'm going to ask the question nobody wants to be asked in 2022. How many hours a day do you spend looking at a screen (phone, tv, computer combined)?

> **❝** CONSUMERS AROUND THE WORLD SPEND AN AVERAGE OF 463 MINUTES OR OVER 7.5 HOURS PER DAY WITH MEDIA. AMERICAN CONSUMERS TEND TO AVERAGE MORE TIME THAN MOST, AS MEDIA IS A MAJOR PART OF THEIR DAILY LIVES. **❞**
>
> –Statista, 2021[xvi]

We have all had that moment when watching a film where we know something from our own life might be triggered by the next scene. Whether it's our spidey senses telling us things are too calm and there's about to be an accident, a gut feeling that we are about to witness a sexual assault or a character's suicide. Trust that. Is watching something that's heavy or a 24/7 news cycle going to energize you and raise your vibes? What about endless scrolling? You get it. I knew you would.

CONSCIOUS EMOTIONAL FITNESS CHECK-IN:

Choose one word in this moment to describe how you are feeling PHYSICALLY, MENTALLY AND EMOTIONALLY.

With AWARENESS of yourself in this moment how do you want to take ACTION?

OFFERING:

CLARITY CLEANSE.

Do a three-day Clarity Cleanse. No technology, no streaming, no digital binging. Just be.

When it gets uncomfortable ask yourself: HOW CAN I BE IN THIS MOMENT?

After the three days, reflect and get conscious the rest of the week about EVERYTHING you are consuming. How do you feel before and after? Notice what you notice. What serves you? How can this awareness be put into action? You get the idea.

Want to Dive Deeper:

- Read *Dopamine Nation* by Dr. Anna Lembke

- Set monthly reminders in your calendar to do a CONSCIOUS CONSUMPTION CHECKS or CLARITY CLEANSES quarterly.

WEEK 21

Keeping busy? Hmm, how busy? Sometimes we fill our schedules and become human doings to not be in the moments of grief and all that we are feeling. If you have been doing this — it's an amazing survival mechanism and you can thank yourself for it now. You can also safely make room this week for what would show up if there was SPACE ... space in your mind, your heart, your calendar, your life.

> **"** WHEN THE WORST HAPPENS, REMEMBER THAT THE ONLY WAY TO STEP OUT OF GRIEF AND SORROW IS TO GIVE YOURSELF TIME TO FULLY STEP INTO IT. NOT IGNORING WHAT YOU FEEL, GIVING IT THE SPACE IT NEEDS, OBSERVING IT WITHOUT REPRESSING IT, IS THE WAY TO ONE DAY MOVE FORWARD AND LIVE AGAIN. **"**

–Yung Pueblo

CONSCIOUS EMOTIONAL FITNESS CHECK-IN:

Choose one word in this moment to describe how you are feeling PHYSICALLY, MENTALLY AND EMOTIONALLY.

With AWARENESS of yourself in this moment how do you want to take ACTION?

OFFERING:

MAKE SPACE.

Make space in your mind, your schedule, and your life this week for natural grief and life to show up as it does without control. Whisper to yourself when you feel the need to fill the time or preschedule/busy yourself.

MAKE SPACE.

SEE WHAT SHOWS UP.

Sometimes what shows up is pure magic.

WEEK 22

Death can be something that we can't stop thinking about or at times want to talk about too much. I have been at a dinner with friends and noticed myself bringing the conversation back to death and my loss. It can come up at very difficult moments and quickly become something we don't want to talk about at all.

Honouring a grief journey gets to come with personal boundaries with both ourselves and others. Are there times when you felt like if you had set a boundary? Maybe you avoided becoming overstimulated, unnecessarily upset, or ending up too far down the rabbit hole of an existential crisis by managing this?

> **"** IN GRIEF, SOME COMMON AREAS THAT CAN REQUIRE BOUNDARIES ARE YOUR TIME, ENERGY, PRIVACY, EMOTIONS, HOME AND BELONGINGS, AND FINANCES. BUT A GOOD PLACE TO START IS TO CONSIDER AREAS WITH FRIENDS, FAMILY, OR COLLEAGUES WHERE YOU HAVE FELT SOME SORT OF TENSION OR RUB SINCE YOUR LOSS. **"**

–What's Your Grief[xvii]

CONSCIOUS EMOTIONAL FITNESS CHECK-IN:

Choose one word in this moment to describe how you are feeling PHYSICALLY, MENTALLY AND EMOTIONALLY.

With AWARENESS of yourself in this moment how do you want to take ACTION?

OFFERING:

BOUNDARIES.

What boundaries would you like to set? Our confidence in boundaries can be built by front-end loading or preparing for when they might come up.

Create a phrase that you can use to respectfully make others aware of boundaries. Here is what I do.

My father died of suicide and people's natural curiosity can lead to me answering questions that are triggering and would require grounding techniques afterwards. So, when it starts to go there, and I don't want to go there, I say something like this:

"As part of my grief journey I have set a boundary around talking about _____ too much, do you mind if we stop here?"

What are your boundaries with yourself? When I start to _____ I will _____.

What are your boundaries with others when it comes to your grief journey?

MY HOPE MONSTER IS HUNGRY.

He needs hope to feed on.

I hold my heart and I say:

I hope I will have the opportunity to love unconditionally again

I hope that I have not hurt the people I love in irreparable ways

I hope my heart stays open and doesn't try to close up

I hope I can be brave

I hope I can be forgiven

I hope I can approach my shame like I do professional challenges

I hope I can live on in loving memories

I hope I can connect people to their hearts

I hope I get the chance to drop from my head into my heart again.

I hope love wins

I hope people stop hating

I hope the stars keep shining, the sun keeps setting, and the moon keeps lighting my path through the darkest of nights

I hope ... to feed my hope monster

CONSCIOUS EMOTIONAL FITNESS CHECK-IN:

Choose one word in this moment to describe how you are feeling PHYSICALLY, MENTALLY AND EMOTIONALLY.

With AWARENESS of yourself in this moment how do you want to take ACTION?

OFFERING:

FEED YOUR
HOPE MONSTER.

Dare to bring hope into your life whenever you can. Yes, this week feed your Hope Monster when it's hungry for hope statements. Say them out loud for your monster to hear and for bonus points. Think of it as building coherence between your brain and your heart.

> **"** A LOVED ONE'S DEATH IS PERMANENT, AND THAT IS SO HEARTBREAKING. BUT I BELIEVE YOUR LOSS OF HOPE CAN BE TEMPORARY. UNTIL YOU CAN FIND IT, I'LL HOLD IT FOR YOU. I HAVE HOPE FOR YOU. I DON'T WANT TO INVALIDATE YOUR FEELINGS AS THEY ARE, BUT I ALSO DON'T WANT TO GIVE DEATH ANY MORE POWER THAN IT ALREADY HAS. DEATH ENDS A LIFE, BUT NOT OUR RELATIONSHIP, OUR LOVE, OR OUR HOPE. **"**

–David Kessler[xviii]

WEEK 24

Do you know the difference between THOUGHTS and FEELINGS?

I have learned that an emotion is a physical state as a result of stimuli. A feeling is your experience of the emotion and its context. A thought is composed of all the words you use to describe it. Our thoughts often skip over labelling the emotion. We say, "I feel like I'm not enough," but really, we are experiencing the emotions of fear and sadness. We then tell ourselves a story about those emotions and what they mean in our life — thoughts about feelings from emotions. Yikes.

CONSCIOUS EMOTIONAL FITNESS CHECK-IN:

Choose one word in this moment to describe how you are feeling PHYSICALLY, MENTALLY AND EMOTIONALLY.

With AWARENESS of yourself in this moment how do you want to take ACTION?

OFFERING:

THOUGHTS VERSUS FEELINGS

Every time you answer the question, "How are you this week?" up the emotional literacy ante and use a more specific combination of FEELING words.

I am willing to admit that at the end of a hard day, I've said to myself or someone else, "I feel like I am not good enough" or "I feel like a failure". I've learned to *pause* at the end of sentences like that. In that pause, I decide if what I just shared was a thought or a feeling.

If it was a thought that I tried to pass off as a feeling, I challenge myself to express what I am actually feeling. For example, I feel like a failure, with more clarity becomes, "I feel tired, worried, my stomach aches and my chest is tight. I feel shame. I feel afraid."

WEEK 25

Six Months. Toolkit check-in.
What's working and perhaps more importantly, what's not?

- Am I checking in daily with how I feel emotionally, mentally and physically?
- Am I allowing silence?
- Am I recording memories and experiences related to my grief?
- Am I breathing?
- Am I trying to control other people?
- Am I accepting my swirl of grief stages and emotions?
- Am I resting?
- Am I speaking and nurturing myself like a child in difficult moments?
- Am I moving?
- Am I affirming anchored with a daily activity?
- Am I measuring or noticing?
- Am I changing my focus before it expands?
- Am I using breath to change my state? Fall asleep? Or calm down?
- Am I allowing gratitude to be a part of my grief journey?
- Am I comparing/competing?
- Am I expressing my anger and other emotions healthily?
- Am I approaching my emotions with beginner eyes and ears?
- Am I allowing feelings of rage to be expressed?
- Am I begging and bargaining when it feels natural?
- Am I sleeping and resting?
- Am I fueling myself with nutrition and hydration?
- Am I listening to music?

- Am I balancing peer and professional support?
- Am I mindful of my triggers?
- Am I consciously consuming with media and screen time?
- Am I making room and seeing what shows up?
- Am I setting and honouring boundaries?
- Am I feeding my hope monster?
- Am I noticing thoughts versus feelings?

THE
SHAME

WEEK 26

What do you NEED? Really. Deep down. Yeah, the soul stuff.

What do you need to honour your journey right now?

I want you to close your eyes for a minute. Take five deep breaths and repeat to yourself:

"I get to feed the darkest parts of me with love."

> **"**ONE ABSOLUTELY CRUCIAL ELEMENT IN MOVING YOUR BRAIN FROM PANIC TO LOGIC IS TO PUT WORDS TO WHAT YOU'RE FEELING AT EACH STAGE.**"**

–Dr. Mark Goulston[xix]

CONSCIOUS EMOTIONAL FITNESS CHECK-IN:

Choose one word in this moment to describe how you are feeling PHYSICALLY, MENTALLY AND EMOTIONALLY.

With AWARENESS of yourself in this moment how do you want to take ACTION?

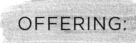

OFFERING:

REACH OUT.

Make a list of three people you trust and let them know what you need right now.

Need help getting the conversation started?

Hey Friend, remember when you said, "If you ever need anything … (at the funeral, when I got fired) … while I'm really feeling _____ I was hoping you could support me this week by _____."

Text, email, call, telegram, post card.

DO IT.

WEEK 27

SOMETIMES IN HONOURING THOSE WE'VE LOST
WE NEED TO ADMIT HOW HURT WE ARE,
AS WEAK AND POWERLESS AS WE MAY FEEL,
OUR HURT IS AN ESSENTIAL PART
OF OUR HUMANITY.

The night I found my father, who died from suicide, I remember standing in the center of that room with everybody staring at me, waiting to hear what I had to say. But for the first time, I had nothing to say at all, I was lost in a place that was quite familiar to me. Every other memory I have in my life involves my senses: what I smelled, tasted ... heard. This particular memory feels more like I was underwater. The sounds and sights are blurred together with no awareness of scents or feelings. I was barely there, yet I was the center of attention. Then, suddenly, my stomach dropped and like a rush I had never felt before, I could feel one distinct thing: wounded. I just stood there.

Do you remember the day you learned of your loss? The moments and hours when your grief process became a reality you couldn't escape?

How do you feel about it now?

CONSCIOUS EMOTIONAL FITNESS CHECK-IN:

Choose one word in this moment to describe how you are feeling PHYSICALLY, MENTALLY AND EMOTIONALLY.

With AWARENESS of yourself in this moment how do you want to take ACTION?

OFFERING:

THE PAST
WITH PERSPECTIVE.

Take some time to get grounded and revisit the moments when you first learned about the loss. Try to do this without referring to your recorded notes I encouraged you to take back on Day 2.

When you think back, what questions comes up?

What limiting beliefs?

What rage or anger?

Anything and everything are welcome. Journal or do a voice memo for yourself. Remember to ground yourself and take time for self-care after this one.

WEEK 28

There are so many times in life where we find ourselves sitting at a fork in the road and in order to continue, we have to make a choice. There are no indicators of where each path will come to, you can only see the first few steps and then after that – who knows.

I used to have a freeze response to these moments, then one day my mentor Jenifer Merifield, introduced me to the idea of FLOW versus FORCE.

Things became simple when I faced a choice and used this question:

What feels like flow and what feels like force?

When it comes to grief, we can unintentionally force showing up in response to loss, in someone's memory or to show we haven't been hurt by a loss.

CONSCIOUS EMOTIONAL FITNESS CHECK-IN:

Choose one word in this moment to describe how you are feeling PHYSICALLY, MENTALLY AND EMOTIONALLY.

With AWARENESS of yourself in this moment how do you want to take ACTION?

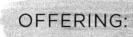

OFFERING:

FLOW VERSUS FORCE

When making choices this week, dig deeper and think about which choices feel like flow and which feels more like force.

What is the choice that gives you a sense of ease, and allows you to be a human be-ing instead of a human do-ing?

What choices feel perfection-driven, controlling, or even as if you are acting for the sake of others.

WEEK 29

Let's talk about prosocial shame. Never heard of it before? Neither had I. Let's get curious about what role shame plays in journey?

Where can you safely show up with your shame?

Prosocial shame is all about having a safe space — a group, or community where you can share your shame and know it will not be judged or define you. Sounds pretty cool right?

In her book *Dopamine Nation*, Dr. Anna Lembke talks about the power of prosocial shame. Here are some of the ideas that really resonated for me and could help you on your grief journey:

1. "Radical honesty promotes awareness, enhances intimacy and fosters a plenty mindset.

2. Prosocial shame affirms that we belong to the human tribe.

3. Instead of running away from the world, we can find escape by immersing ourselves in it."[xx]

CONSCIOUS EMOTIONAL FITNESS CHECK-IN:

Choose one word in this moment to describe how you are feeling PHYSICALLY, MENTALLY AND EMOTIONALLY.

With AWARENESS of yourself in this moment how do you want to take ACTION?

OFFERING:

COMMUNITY.

Find one new group of people that the person you lost never knew before and neither did you. It is a supportive, new perspective community. Join a group, meetups.com, etc.

Community had been the glue of my life as I bounced around from one mental health professional to the other looking to be fixed instead of accepting and processing my grief. When I found myself at the point of suicidal depression, it was my community who saved me.

> **"** WHEN WE SEEK FOR CONNECTION, WE
> RESTORE THE WORLD TO WHOLENESS, OUR
> SEEMINGLY SEPARATE LIVES BECOME MEANINGFUL
> AS WE REALIZE HOW NECESSARY WE ARE TO EACH
> OTHER. **"**

–Margaret Wheatley[xxi]

WEEK 30

Let's get intentional and carve out some quality time to remember what and who has been lost this week. Maybe you have felt that in your gut, your chest, or your throat. Where do you carry your loss most as a bodily experience? Think about breathing into that place when you are intentionally remembering them.

Sometimes we can look at a piece of art, sit in a theater, or be reading something and suddenly feel a sting in our heart and be out of breath. *Whoever gets this, gets me.*

"IN REALITY, THERE IS A BIOLOGY OF GRIEF AND LOSS THAT INVOLVES TRANSFORMATION OF ACTIONABLE STEPS (THE DESIRE TO CALL SOMEONE, LAUGH WITH THEM, HOLD THEM) INTO NON-ACTIONABLE THOUGHTS. THAT TRANSFORMATION = GRIEF. "

–Dr. Andrew Huberman[xxii]

CONSCIOUS EMOTIONAL FITNESS CHECK-IN:

Choose one word in this moment to describe how you are feeling PHYSICALLY, MENTALLY AND EMOTIONALLY.

With AWARENESS of yourself in this moment how do you want to take ACTION?

REMEMBER.

Pick a poem, passage or quote that reminds you of who you lost. It might feel like it has been a while since we took the time to talk about and remember them. It feels like people have moved on, yet that isn't true. Read it daily this week. See how it feels different each time and what comes up.

Email it to me: share@mygriefclub.com

I mean it. Let's honour them together.

WEEK 31

When was the last time you laughed? Like really, really, laughed. The kind where your stomach aches and your eyes water and you live in the freedom that it's okay to feel that much joy in any given moment.

> **"HUMOR IS ALSO IMPORTANT DURING THE TIME OF GRIEVING. WHEN WE ARE IN THE DEPTHS OF DESPAIR OVER THE LOSS OF OUR LOVED ONE, IT IS HARD TO THINK THAT WE WILL EVER SMILE AGAIN LET ALONE LAUGH. ONE OF THE TASKS OF GRIEVING IS TO LEARN TO LAUGH AGAIN."**
>
> –Dr. Marilyn A Mendoza[xxiii]

So, who is that one person who always makes you laugh? That one comedian? That one movie? Shall we head to the "find the funny" section of the grief arena and play a little?

Follow me.

CONSCIOUS EMOTIONAL FITNESS CHECK-IN:

Choose one word in this moment to describe how you are feeling PHYSICALLY, MENTALLY AND EMOTIONALLY.

With AWARENESS of yourself in this moment how do you want to take ACTION?

OFFERING:

LAUGH 'TIL YOU CRY.

Find the funny this week. It can be in direct relation to your grief or a total escape, but this week's experiment is to see how much you can laugh and how it helps.

Make a list of what and who you find funny here. Sometimes when life changes, our humor does to. I hate to say the overused term "lean in" but, lean in!

DR. MARK GOULSTON:

Well, the point is, that's all normal. You know life is like an 88 key, you know, piano keyboard, and you've got to play every key once, at least once. But I wanted to share that because a lot of times people in grief really have trouble admitting or accepting the level of rage that they felt like a reaction to the hurt and fear. And that can offer in the shame of feeling it so deeply. Oh, I'm a bad person, you know, I'm not in grief. I'm in rage now. That's all part of it. So I wanted to share that because I think that's something that a number of people in grief stumble over, and it's just part of. It's just part of playing all the keys on that keyboard.

ADDISON:

I mean, that is definitely going to bleed into this
book that I'm writing. I mean that so beautifully
    said, and I feel like we have so many rites of
    passage set up in that early part of life. And
    like that is such for anyone listening. I mean,
    it's uncomfortable. It makes us. We're all going
    to die one day and we're all going to grieve one
    day. So if there's that opportunity to give your
children your loved ones, whomever that permission
  to grieve fully, to grieve you for everything that
                comes with that.

My Wake Up Call With Dr. Mark Goulston ft. Addison Brasil

WEEK 32

Survivor's Guilt. Take a moment before I say anything to breathe into that term and think about what it means for you. Is it a part of your journey or something that doesn't align at all? No wrong answers in grief.

Are there certain activities, experiences or even physical abilities that make you feel guilty?

Without judgement, take a moment and list out anything that has made you feel guilty or that thinking about doing now makes you feel guilty?

CONSCIOUS EMOTIONAL FITNESS CHECK-IN:

Choose one word in this moment to describe how you are feeling PHYSICALLY, MENTALLY AND EMOTIONALLY.

With AWARENESS of yourself in this moment how do you want to take ACTION?

OFFERING:

GO THERE.

Not just mentally this week, but go there physically. Go to one new place that they never knew or never went. Be fully in an experience without them and notice how you feel. Don't judge what does or doesn't come up, just honour it.

WHEN YOU "GO THERE" – MAKE A CONSCIOUS
EFFORT TO TAP IN YOUR 5 SENSES.
CHALLENGE YOURSELF NOT TO DECIDE HOW
THE EXPERIENCE IS GOING UNTIL ITS OVER.
FOCUS ON FEELINGS, NOT THOUGHTS.
THIS CAN BE A VERY GENTLE AND HONEST
PROCESS. AS THOUGHTS AND FEAR SHOW UP,
SMILE, BREATHE AND RE DIRECT YOURSELF
BACK TO YOUR SENSES.

WEEK 33

"EVERYTHING IS JUST DIFFERENT NOW."

"THIS ISN'T HOW IT WAS SUPPOSED TO BE"

Sometimes we get caught up in life comparisons and in a way, it is a part of our very human need to bargain before accepting change.

My mentor once gifted me the opportunity to consider the world, people, and situations with beginner's eyes and ears.

She encouraged me to approach it as if it was the first time I was seeing or hearing.

Try it. Even if you use something your parent, friend or sibling has said a million times before this moment. If all that preconceived tension and energy were not present, what do you hear and see?

CONSCIOUS EMOTIONAL FITNESS CHECK-IN:

Choose one word in this moment to describe how you are feeling PHYSICALLY, MENTALLY AND EMOTIONALLY.

With AWARENESS of yourself in this moment how do you want to take ACTION?

OFFERING:

BEGINNER
EYES AND EARS.

This week, every time you find yourself in a conversation or an interaction with another living being (pets count too), approach it with beginner's eyes and ears.

A week of firsts.

How do you show up when you listen and see from the new perspective you've built in the last 33 weeks?

Keep notes when these opportunities come up.

Old Self would have:

New Self got to:

WEEK 34

How often do you feel grounded? We often think that being grounded is the same as being "normal", as though it's something that happens when we are not grieving or suffering. In actuality, grounding is part of a daily practice and there are badass practitioners all over the world who have come up with some amazing techniques to do it.

Some of my favorites include planting my bare feet in sand or grass and being present with nature, tapping techniques, tuning into my senses, and even nose breathing for ten minutes at a time.

CONSCIOUS EMOTIONAL FITNESS CHECK-IN:

Choose one word in this moment to describe how you are feeling PHYSICALLY, MENTALLY AND EMOTIONALLY.

With AWARENESS of yourself in this moment how do you want to take ACTION?

OFFERING:

GET GROUNDED.

Choose one daily grounding technique to do every day for seven days that puts you in the safety of the present moment.

Notice how you feel before and after a grounding technique. Rate your overwhelm or state of calm on a scale from 1 to 10 each time and record it. Make sure to record before and after.

WEEK 35

"I want to feel healthy again" or "I just want to be healthy" can be something that comes up on this journey. Sometimes we find ourselves saying things like this without defining for ourselves what exactly "healthy", "well" or "thriving " mean to us.

It's like saying you're hungry at a restaurant but then not choosing an item on the menu. Do you want someone else to decide the definition of these vital elements of our life and grief journey? Probably not.

CONSCIOUS EMOTIONAL FITNESS CHECK-IN:

Choose one word in this moment to describe how you are feeling PHYSICALLY, MENTALLY AND EMOTIONALLY.

With AWARENESS of yourself in this moment how do you want to take ACTION?

OFFERING:

DEFINE HEALTH.

This week take time to think and then define what the word HEALTH means to you. Write it down and tune into how this definition of health can become a reality in your life.

I'm happy to share mine for inspiration: Health is my optimal and natural state of being where I am presently choosing within my life to serve my nutrition, energy levels, emotional and physical fitness. It is the absence of inflammation and pain.

WEEK 36

CHECKING IN

- Am I checking in daily with how I feel emotionally, mentally and physically?
- Am I allowing silence?
- Am I recording memories and experiences related to my grief?
- Am I breathing?
- Am I trying to control other people?
- Am I accepting my swirl of grief stages and emotions?
- Am I resting?
- Am I speaking and nurturing myself like a child in difficult moments?
- Am I moving?
- Am I affirming anchored with a daily activity?
- Am I measuring or noticing?
- Am I changing my focus before it expands?
- Am I using breath to change my state? Fall asleep? Or calm down?
- Am I allowing gratitude to be a part of my grief journey?
- Am I comparing/competing?
- Am I expressing my anger and other emotions healthily?
- Am I approaching my emotions with beginner eyes and ears?
- Am I allowing feelings of rage to be expressed?
- Am I begging and bargaining when it feels natural?
- Am I sleeping and resting?
- Am I fueling myself with nutrition and hydration?
- Am I listening to music?
- Am I balancing peer and professional support?

- Am I mindful of my triggers?
- Am I consciously consuming with media and screen time?
- Am I making room and seeing what shows up?
- Am I setting and honouring boundaries?
- Am I feeding my hope monster?
- Am I noticing thoughts versus feelings?
- Am I reaching out?
- Am I avoiding the past/new perspective?
- Am I in a state of flow or force?
- Am I investing in community?
- Am I remembering them?
- Am I laughing?
- Am I aware of survivor's guilt?
- Am I finding ways that work for me to get grounded?
- Am I conscious of my own definition of health?

THE
SURRENDER

WEEK 37

Sometimes when we hear about a concept or healing modality for the first time we want to dive deeper in order to get that "I'm in" feeling. Then the novelty wears off, and when we don't follow through, we feel silly or at worst shameful about returning to the idea or modality for healing.

Fuck that. Yes, I swore.

And yes, I am bringing shame up again, cause one weekly experiment is not going to do it. We are humans, with years of programming and beliefs working against us. Shame showing up is universal. How it shows up is specific to you.

CONSCIOUS EMOTIONAL FITNESS CHECK-IN:

Choose one word in this moment to describe how you are feeling PHYSICALLY, MENTALLY AND EMOTIONALLY.

With AWARENESS of yourself in this moment how do you want to take ACTION?

OFFERING:

GET SPECIFIC.

Earlier in our grief sibling relationship I invited you to say, whisper or even announce to the world what you needed or wanted to bring into your life and to anchor it to something you do every day. How's that been going? If it's been going well, I invite you to clarify the affirmation and get more specific. See what happens next. If you haven't been, I want to gently invite you to try it again. Even if it's as simple as saying I love you to yourself when you first see your reflection each day.

It's just an experiment. Doing this doesn't make you a woo-woo manifester of magic and automatically sign you up for a soul retreat in Sedona. I promise.

What do you need to hear right now?

WEEK 38

At times in my grief process, I have felt ways that I couldn't describe using English words or passages in books. Even with the some 171,000 words in the English language, there are many experiences and feelings that are only describable by other languages. Untranslatables can go unsaid but not un-felt. I want you to know you are not alone in the in-between moments.

Saudade is a Portuguese word meaning a deep emotional state of nostalgic or profound melancholic longing for something or someone that one cares for and/or loves. Moreover, it often carries a repressed knowledge that the object of longing might never be had again.

I had to come up with language on my own such as "THE SWIRL" or "mooshy" or even "dippy eggs." Dippy eggs for me was a play on how my mom used to make us eggs that were safely cooked but the yolk was still runny for us to dip our toast in. To me it meant to my friends and family, I'm safe but my grief, or yolk, was vulnerable with the slightest touch.

CONSCIOUS EMOTIONAL FITNESS CHECK-IN:

Choose one word in this moment to describe how you are feeling PHYSICALLY, MENTALLY AND EMOTIONALLY.

With AWARENESS of yourself in this moment how do you want to take ACTION?

OFFERING:

NO WORDS.

Allow what cannot be defined or explained this week to just be. Allow its authenticity to be within your be-ing. Even if there are things you can't explain to anyone, not a friend, coach, therapist, or practitioner ... take a deep breath and feel into it. Honour your untranslatables.

DEEPER DIVE:

Read *They Have a Word for It: Lighthearted Lexicon of Untranslatable Words & Phrases* by Howard Rheingold

WEEK 39

How often do you find yourself saying the words NEED TO, HAVE TO or SHOULD?

Yeah, take a deep breath and a moment to really sit with that. Be honest, it's just us.

Close your eyes for a moment. Put one hand on your heart and one hand on your stomach. Breathe deeply in through your nose for five seconds and exhale until all the air leaves your body. Imagine for a moment while listening to your breath and heartbeat what it would be like to not feel like you need to, have to or should do anything. Breathe deeply into the feeling it brings up.

CONSCIOUS EMOTIONAL FITNESS CHECK-IN:

Choose one word in this moment to describe how you are feeling PHYSICALLY, MENTALLY AND EMOTIONALLY.

With AWARENESS of yourself in this moment how do you want to take ACTION?

OFFERING:

GET TO.

This week every time you say a sentence with the words "need to" "have to" or "should" stop and replace the words with "get to." Notice the magic that ensues, how it feels differently and how it serves you.

"It's important to touch into the space of non-striving.

What is it like to just be? To not be caught in the story of who you are, where you're going, what you need to accomplish?

If we never touch into this space of being, to experience what it's like to live beyond ideas, then it's easy to assume that striving is all there is, and is all there should be.
That we should always be trying to get some place else, always be trying to improve, and never settling.

Is there something more, though?

Is there a way to achieve, accomplish and produce without burden?

What if you could live in the world expressing yourself from a place of inspiration and freedom, rather than being shackled to your mental narrative of how you need to live, or worse yet, someone else's narrative of how you need to live?

When we truly stop, we feel into all of the stories that have been pulling and pushing our being. Only in that space of non-striving can we taste the early stages of freedom, and connect with a deeper, internal source of how to navigate life with that freedom."

— Cory Muscara[xxiv]

WEEK 40

Birthdays, learning new things, life events and even promotions are meant to be celebrated, but in the wake of a loss doing so can make us feel like we are growing apart from those we've lost.

Limiting beliefs start to form:

"If I stay the same as I was the day I lost them then I will stay close to them."

"I don't want to become someone that they didn't know."

CONSCIOUS EMOTIONAL FITNESS CHECK-IN:

Choose one word in this moment to describe how you are feeling PHYSICALLY, MENTALLY AND EMOTIONALLY.

With AWARENESS of yourself in this moment how do you want to take ACTION?

OFFERING:

WITHOUT THEM.

This week, get on YouTube, book an AirBnB Experience, find a book in a section you'd typically never explore and learn something new. Test your resistance level to evolving WITHOUT THEM. It is a (super)power to know where you are at. Great power comes with great responsibility, Spidey. You got this.

We fear being alone, not because of loneliness, but because we'll have no choice but to listen to our true thoughts, and more importantly, have no one to answer to but ourselves.

> **EMOTIONS ARE BUILT ON LAYERS. BENEATH HATRED IS USUALLY ANGER; BENEATH ANGER IS FRUSTRATION; BENEATH FRUSTRATION IS HURT; BENEATH HURT IS FEAR. IF YOU KEEP EXPRESSING YOUR FEELINGS, YOU WILL GENERALLY MOVE THROUGH THEM IN THAT ORDER. WHAT BEGINS WITH "I HATE YOU" CULMINATES IN "I'M SCARED. I DON'T WANT TO LOSE YOU, AND I DON'T KNOW WHAT TO DO ABOUT IT.**

–Mark Goulston[xxv]

David Vox:
So, you surrendered?

Addison Brasil:
Surrendered, exactly. And that's ...
One of the S's that I play with in my book is that, surrendering. There's a lot of other S's and maybe another S word that comes before, before you get to that surrendering. It's just very scary, because I used to always have this question in my head like, "What happens to the third Brasil boy?" Meaning, my brother and my father, and then I'm this third boy in the Brasil family. And what happens? And I learned that summer, in that suicidal depression, that he dies, too. Everything I knew and believed in the operating system, he had to die. There was no way I could carry forward what I thought life should be with what life now was. There was just no way. And I literally kind of had to let every part of my defence mechanism die.

From Love Gladiator Podcast with David Vox "Letting The Loss Live: Honouring The Grief Inside Us With Addison Brasil"

WEEK 41

Sometimes, in trying to be polite or feel normal again we fall into just giving up on trying to get people to understand our grief journey and what it really means to be a part of Grief Club.

Frustration, shame, anger, revengeful thoughts are all part of this mixed tape we never wanted to be gifted in the first place.

From experience I can say that if these thoughts and feelings don't have an outlet, they tend to find their way out and the most in opportune moments.

Like a volcano that erupts, once certain feelings and thoughts are pushed down – from the outside there is no way to know when they might show up again.

For me, this happened months after the loss of my dad, someone at a local store was really not doing their best when it came to customer service and my response had nothing to do with that store. Oh yes, whatever you are picturing, magnify it by ten. I went there and it suddenly became their fault — all of it.

CONSCIOUS EMOTIONAL FITNESS CHECK-IN:

Choose one word in this moment to describe how you are feeling PHYSICALLY, MENTALLY AND EMOTIONALLY.

With AWARENESS of yourself in this moment how do you want to take ACTION?

OFFERING:

VENT.

" AS LONG AS YOU KEEP SECRETS
AND SUPPRESS INFORMATION, YOU ARE
FUNDAMENTALLY AT WAR WITH YOURSELF...THE
CRITICAL ISSUE IS ALLOWING YOURSELF TO KNOW
WHAT YOU KNOW. THAT TAKES AN ENORMOUS
AMOUNT OF COURAGE. **"**

–Bessel A. van der Kolk[xxvi]

In writing my memoir, I was regularly bombarded by thoughts of including many things that were part of my journey but decided not to out of respect for others, privacy and general hope for human kind. The more I *pushed* those parts of my story down the less I was able to write around them. Finally, my book coach suggested that I make a separate locked secure document and write out all the things I felt I could never share or say to anyone. I called it The Stories I'm Not Allowed to Tell.

The offering is to find your version of this, whether it's in the extra gray space at the end of this book, in a separate book that can be kept in a safe or even burned, or a secure document — write out the things that reading the last two pages ignited in you. Yeah, that stuff. It's just for you to know. With this awareness, you can take action, set boundaries, find flow and hopefully feel freedom from the shame of what can't be said.

There is nothing in Grief Club that is shameful to share. Not one thing.

WEEK 42

There are a lot of amazing resources when it comes to grief. The "grief giants" who study and write on grief have shown up in incredible ways to create books, podcasts, retreats, workshops and ongoing support groups.

I found in all three of my grief journeys, that I wasn't ready to approach or "study" grief until much later. If I read certain books too early, what was meant to ease me into the normalcy of grief felt like being told that I was about to have the worst year of my life and it already felt bad enough. With time, perspective, and spending my own time in the grief arena with fellow club members, I did get a lot of value from exploring grief as a subject.

CONSCIOUS EMOTIONAL FITNESS CHECK-IN:

Choose one word in this moment to describe how you are feeling PHYSICALLY, MENTALLY AND EMOTIONALLY.

With AWARENESS of yourself in this moment how do you want to take ACTION?

OFFERING:

GRIEF GIANTS.

Use the gray space below to list any books, podcasts etc that you've turned to in attempting to understand loss or grief:

Now, choose one book or podcast that you would think will truly serve you when it comes to beginning to explore a sense of purpose and meaning within your grief?

What are you craving?

What do you need to know to move forward from this exact moment in your grief process?

WEEK 43

In the book *Wise as Fu*k*, Gary John Bishop talks about loss in a new and beautiful way:

It can be from "A life put on hold or taking a wild turn or waiting for a change that ultimately never comes. Regret. Disappointment. Sometimes Resentment too."[xvii]

He goes on to talk about the other losses we grapple with in life that we may not be tending to or even acknowledging.

"Maybe your marriage or relationship hasn't gone the way you expected, perhaps it's that job or house or plan that would have solved all your shit. Maybe the dream of your best-selling book you had been longing for and fantasizing over hasn't quite manifested in the cold reality of your life, all the way down to the depths of the childhood you deserved, never quite matching up to the one you got."

I call these micro grief processes. Micro does not refer to them being small and invalid. It is in reference to the idea that sometimes we have to be curious and compassionate enough to take out a microscope and acknowledge what's under the surfaces; the losses along the way that got over looked.

CONSCIOUS EMOTIONAL FITNESS CHECK-IN:

Choose one word in this moment to describe how you are feeling PHYSICALLY, MENTALLY AND EMOTIONALLY.

With AWARENESS of yourself in this moment how do you want to take ACTION?

OFFERING:

THE 'LITTLE' LOSSES.

Take time to notice the other grieving you're doing this week. Honour the micro grief processes you are dealing with. What else has changed?

Make a list of the other grief you've dealt with; the losses of anything meaningful. This experiment is not intended to create a heavy cloud of grief awareness. As you go through, notice what helped with the grief that came up in the past and what needs the most attention in the present moment.

Do any of them bring up Regret, Disappointment or Resentment, or all three? This is a good thing to know. If yes, how would you like to approach exploring these feelings? If at all.

WEEK 44

You have just gotten underground to ride the train and reach for your earphones to listen to your favorite podcast and … you have forgotten them. Or you finally get yourself to the gym and climb onto the spin bike only to realize you don't have headphones and it's just not the same without the epic workout songs that get you through.

Cue the World Is Against Me Victim Mindset-style thinking. We have all been there.

What if you interrupted that "ever since my loss things just keep piling on" mindset with … Wait. Hold on. What is this the perfect opportunity for? Perhaps you are meant to hear something right now. Perhaps it's the perfect time to see how navigating discomfort almost always leads to personal growth. Who knows?

CONSCIOUS EMOTIONAL FITNESS CHECK-IN:

Choose one word in this moment to describe how you are feeling PHYSICALLY, MENTALLY AND EMOTIONALLY.

With AWARENESS of yourself in this moment how do you want to take ACTION?

OFFERING:

WHAT IS THIS, REALLY.

When things don't go "as planned" this week see each time as its own opportunity to ask, "What is this the perfect opportunity for?" and answer that question wholeheartedly. If you play along that everything is for your benefit in some way, what happens?

> **" I URGE YOU TO FIND A WAY TO IMMERSE YOURSELF FULLY IN THE LIFE THAT YOU'VE BEEN GIVEN. TO STOP RUNNING FROM WHATEVER YOU'RE TRYING TO ESCAPE, AND INSTEAD TO STOP, AND TURN, AND FACE WHATEVER IT IS. "**

–Anna Lembke[xxviii]

THE
SHOW UP

WEEK 45

I will never forget the first time I heard the terms grief-adjacent and grief-stricken. Grief does not discriminate and it will find anyone who connects, loves, dreams, hopes, tries and fails. We are not alone in this and yet, it can be so isolating.

David Kessler drives this home even more when doing interviews saying, "Love and grief are a package deal on planet earth."

CONSCIOUS EMOTIONAL FITNESS CHECK-IN:

Choose one word in this moment to describe how you are feeling PHYSICALLY, MENTALLY AND EMOTIONALLY.

With AWARENESS of yourself in this moment how do you want to take ACTION?

OFFERING:

YOUR TURN.

What experiments would you suggest for someone who is freshly transitioning from being grief-adjacent to grief-stricken?

If you were to write the next Grief Club book, what would you want to add for our fellow travelers?

Want to dive deeper, share your grief thoughts here.

> **GRIEF, I'VE LEARNED, IS REALLY JUST LOVE. IT'S ALL THE LOVE YOU WANT TO GIVE BUT CANNOT. ALL OF THAT UNSPENT LOVE GATHERS UP IN THE CORNERS OF YOUR EYES, THE LUMP IN YOUR THROAT, AND IN THAT HOLLOW PART OF YOUR CHEST. GRIEF IS JUST LOVE WITH NO PLACE TO GO.**

–Jamie Anderson[xxix]

WEEK 46

Let's remember them.

Pick a piece of art, a spot in nature, something you can show up to with all of your senses. If you live life without one of your senses, focus deeper on what you do feel.

I repeat this stage because every so often it feels like we have all forgotten, started to live in a world without _____. It might feel like a good time to consciously carve out some time to talk about them and remember.

> " MOST OF THE CONVERSATIONS THAT WE HAVE IN THE (SUPPORT) GROUP CAN AND WILL JUST STAY AMONGST OURSELVES, BUT THERE ARE THINGS THAT WE TALK ABOUT THAT THE REST OF THE WORLD – THE WORLD THAT IS GRIEF-ADJACENT BUT NOT YET GRIEF-STRICKEN – COULD REALLY BENEFIT FROM HEARING. "
>
> –Nora McInerny[xxxi]

CONSCIOUS EMOTIONAL FITNESS CHECK-IN:

Choose one word in this moment to describe how you are feeling PHYSICALLY, MENTALLY AND EMOTIONALLY.

With AWARENESS of yourself in this moment how do you want to take ACTION?

OFFERING:

REMEMBER TO REMEMBER.

Make a plan around spending time with this place in nature or in the presence of this art as much as you can this week. See how it feels different each time and what comes up. Email it to me I mean it, let's honour them together.

share@mygriefclub.com

WEEK 47

I could have told you in our first week together that there is no PERFECT way to grieve. I might have said that 'trying to be perfect would only harm you,' but I feel like as a fellow grief sibling in the arena, I can just sort of bring that up now and let you come to your own conclusions.

In the experiments and offerings this year where did trying to be perfect really help?

Let's use some gray space to jot down our gut reaction to that?

CONSCIOUS EMOTIONAL FITNESS CHECK-IN:

Choose one word in this moment to describe how you are feeling PHYSICALLY, MENTALLY AND EMOTIONALLY.

With AWARENESS of yourself in this moment how do you want to take ACTION?

PERFECTION VERSUS EXCELLENCE

This week, notice when you are trying to perfect (with force and fear) your experience and when you are approaching it from an excellence (flow and love-based) mindset. The experiences that fall under perfection — notice how they feel. The experiences that fall under excellence — notice how they feel. From the awareness build actionable tools.

WEEK 48

When we first lose someone or something meaningful, no one tells us this comes with a to do list. Unsaid duties of dealing with grief around death can include cleaning out the closet, responding to the will, addressing the things that have been sitting like the DMV, the memberships, the mail, their shoes and coats that are still in the front closet in case they come home any minute … yeah. Deep breath. We got this.

The truth is some of these things aren't just taking up physical space, they are taking up emotional and mental energy. Sometimes avoiding or ignoring can be more force than flow. If this is resonating, then one thing, or seven things, are probably coming up in your mind right now.

CONSCIOUS EMOTIONAL FITNESS CHECK-IN:

Choose one word in this moment to describe how you are feeling PHYSICALLY, MENTALLY AND EMOTIONALLY.

With AWARENESS of yourself in this moment how do you want to take ACTION?

REAL LIFE GRIEF GET TO'S.

Write down the "SHOULD do" list. Which of course, we know is a "get to" list. Then take the list and put (in order) the things you feel most ready to deal with at the top and things you feel least ready to take on at the bottom. Do the first thing. Bonus points if you breathe and stay present through doing it, but let's not get wild. How did doing it feel? Would you like to clear some more emotional space that maybe could be used for love? Let's go to the next item on this list.

P.S. If you are physically getting rid of anything, feel free to take pictures of the items first.

GRIEF IS THE LOSS OF ANYTHING MEANINGFUL

WEEK 49

> **" YOUR LOSS IS NOT A TEST, A LESSON, SOMETHING TO HANDLE, A GIFT, OR A BLESSING. LOSS IS SIMPLY WHAT HAPPENS TO YOU IN LIFE. MEANING IS WHAT YOU MAKE HAPPEN. "**

–David Kessler

Take a moment and decide if this quote resonates with you. It comes from David Kessler's book *Finding Meaning, The Sixth Stage of Grief* (2019). When we get to know our grief and truly honour it, sometimes it can become the seed of something new — something that aligns with our purpose and brings meaning to our lives. It is also perfectly okay if it doesn't, if it just is what it is.

For me, my brother's death turned into a 14-year non-profit mission called Team Brother Bear that supports families who are caring for a child living with a brain tumor. In memory of my dad, I felt I inherited the responsibility of investing and educating myself about mental health, which eventually led to me co-founding the world's first peer support brand for men; tethr. When my friend passed, I just had to survive. I felt like my old operating system didn't work and meaning and purpose were fleeing fast. So, I nurtured myself and remained curious and self-compassionate about what would bring me purpose next.

As always there are no rules.

CONSCIOUS EMOTIONAL FITNESS CHECK-IN:

Choose one word in this moment to describe how you are feeling PHYSICALLY, MENTALLY AND EMOTIONALLY.

With AWARENESS of yourself in this moment how do you want to take ACTION?

OFFERING:

PURPOSE AND MEANING.

This week, in between the silence and the swirls, the surrenders and the survivor moments think about what makes you want to show up. When I say show up, I mean what inspires you right now to get involved and bring all of yourself to it.

It may be a completely new passion or purpose from before the loss occurred. Sometimes we resist this, because we don't want to change too much from when we lost someone or something so important to us. Another perspective might be that all that "love with nowhere to go" finds a new project or hobby or career to fuel.

As always, it's up to you. Going to leave a lot of gray space for this one.

"What would best honor the years they didn't get? That could be one way of bringing meaning to our lives without them."

– David Kessler

WEEK 50

When I ask you, "Do you love yourself?" what comes up?

Raw and unfiltered set a timer for ten minutes and just write, draw or speak out loud and even consider how you might explain this idea to a child:

> **"** SELF-LOVE DOESN'T MEAN WE DON'T SEE ROOM FOR GROWTH; IT JUST MEANS THAT OUR FEELINGS OF WORTHINESS ARE NOT CONTINGENT UPON THAT GROWTH. SELF-LOVE THAT IS PREDICATED UPON REACHING AND MAINTAINING A CERTAIN VERSION OF OURSELVES IS AN INCOMPLETE SELF-LOVE. **"**
>
> –Cory Muscara

CONSCIOUS EMOTIONAL FITNESS CHECK-IN:

Choose one word in this moment to describe how you are feeling PHYSICALLY, MENTALLY AND EMOTIONALLY.

With AWARENESS of yourself in this moment how do you want to take ACTION?

OFFERING:

LOVE ON YOURSELF.

This one is not easy for most of us but I have learned the hard way that it is an integral part of stepping into resilience and even finding joy, awe and hope within our grief journeys.

This week I want to challenge you to start to recognize, in every choice you make, what feels like love and what doesn't.

It can be as simple as what you choose to eat or drink. What you watch on Netflix or YouTube. How you choose to start your day. How you talk to yourself, both out loud and in your head. Just get really curious about what feels like self-love and what doesn't.

You may have come up with a lot of thoughts and feelings about self-love on the previous page, or it might still just be gray space. Gray space is full of possibilities.

When I _____ I feel like I am loving myself.

You choose.

Don't overthink it.

What makes you feel empowered, held, comfortable but not stuck?

WEEK 51

I BELIEVE EVERYTHING DOES NOT HAPPEN FOR A REASON, BUT YOU CAN BE THE REASON EVERYTHING STILL HAPPENS.

After years of people smiling at me awkwardly and innocently saying, "Everything happens for a reason," one day I finally responded organically with the above sentiment.

I was once challenged and invited by master coach and my mentor, Jenifer Merifield to revisit my traumatic losses with a new perspective.

"In a world where you can't change the past or save people from death, but everything serves you in you some way … what can you privately and honestly say you have learned."

At first, I hated the idea and didn't want to play into any sort of "everything happens for reason" logic. After a few days I reapproached what I call The Benefit Game. I call it a game because I still tiptoe around the idea of believing there could be benefits from my losses.

I realized how much I had grown and how much more emotionally intelligent I had become. I could see how being supported had allowed me to support so many others without conditions or expectations. I realized that I have raised thousands of dollars and brought together thousands of people for social impact causes. Mostly, I realized I had become an empathic, wholehearted person whose wealth is the many deeply connected relationships I formed in my young adult life. My time in the arena was a constant practice of loving and being loved.

CONSCIOUS EMOTIONAL FITNESS CHECK-IN:

Choose one word in this moment to describe how you are feeling PHYSICALLY, MENTALLY AND EMOTIONALLY.

With AWARENESS of yourself in this moment how do you want to take ACTION?

OFFERING:

PLAY THE BENEFIT GAME.

Just for one hour this week set a timer and play The Benefit Game. List out your losses and just for that one hour write down anything that comes to mind that was in service to you because you experienced these losses. What did you learn? How did you grow?

Remember, this does not make it okay that you lost someone or something deeply meaningful to you. It does not wipe away your grief, make it easier or diminish it in any way.

Don't want to? Don't. As always, it's just a deeper experiment. And it will be here today or years from now, right on this page. There's no time limit.

ONE YEAR

On the yearly anniversaries of my losses I have a ritual of finding the biggest body of water I can and watching the sunset over it. What started out in 2009 as a tearful memorial for my brother has become something I look forward to and do more often than once a year. This tradition has become an integrity check for me.

I used to hear the word integrity and think it was based on someone else's judgement of my character. I came to learn that the word integrity evolved from the Latin adjective integer meaning whole or complete and something clicked in me. The fastest way I find myself back in integrity is with deep breathing. I connect with the parts of my body that are physically keeping me alive, my heart and my lungs, and then return to what I was moving through.

Wholeness and completeness occur for me when I can be in awareness of my whole being – mentally, emotionally, physically and spiritually. When action comes from that awareness – it's almost always in integrity.

The whole and complete picture are a part of that. It is in acceptance of my losses, my triumphs, my failures, my hopes, my lack and my love. It's not about showing resilience, it's about *being* resilience. It doesn't put shiny parts forward to hide what is still healing – it just is.

All of it and all of me, in our entirety.

CONSCIOUS EMOTIONAL FITNESS CHECK-IN:

Choose one word in this moment to describe how you are feeling PHYSICALLY, MENTALLY AND EMOTIONALLY.

With AWARENESS of yourself in this moment how do you want to take ACTION?

OFFERING:

HONOUR YOUR YEAR.

For some of us New Year's Eve only acknowledges the change in a calendar year. Our grief journeys aren't always aligned with linear time and certainly cannot be lined up with January 1st each year.

Set your own ritual to find a safe space and honour this moment. Let it be a time to reflect, remember, align and self-soothe. Give yourself permission to celebrate the curiosity, compassion and self-kindness that you have begun to delicately weave into your grief journey.

Within this experience, after a year of experiments, take a moment to update your personal definition of grief. What has evolved since first starting grief club?

EPILOGUE

I intended to use this space to fill in the gaps and tidy up what this book should have helped you do and learn, but only two words come to mind: **you know.**

I hope *you know* the power of staying curious, compassionate and kind.

I hope *you know* your silence, your swirl, your survival, your shame, your surrender and your show up matter.

I hope *you know* that you get to build a new relationship with grief every day.

I hope *you know* what serves you and what doesn't.

I hope *you know* your hope monster more intimately, and have a few more ways to answer when your hope monster is starving.

I hope *you know* what honour-ing your journey feels like, looks like, tastes like.

I hope *you know* I trust you.

I hope *you know* whatever does or doesn't happen next, is up to you.

I hope *you know Grief Club* is for life and we can live fully within it.

I hope *you know* I am somewhere waiting to hear from you, how this went, how I could have supported you more, and what your offerings are, if any, for the Grief Club arena in return.

You know that you choose your next experiment.

And if you don't know, you can come back here for the reminders from one member of Grief Club to another.

Honour the journey,

Addison

AFTERWORD

In November of 2021, I wrote this out of a beautiful and wild mixture of grief and gratitude on the breakfast porch at Modern Elder Academy located in Baja, California Sur, Mexico.

> ## *"I Baja-ed It!"*
>
> A year of nomading and grieving.
>
> A year of honoring and not fixing.
>
> A year of active and empathic listening.
>
> A year of loving, not just others, but myself.
>
> A year of powerful badassery.
>
> A year exploring and navigating being Just to the Left of Death three times.
>
> And so I went …
>
> I went to Greece in honor of my brother's wish before he passed of Cancer.
>
> I went to Italy to eat and celebrate my late friend.
>
> I went to Austin to innovate.
>
> I went to Palm Springs for inclusion and to mend my heart.
>
> I went to Canada to see my family and build with passion.
>
> I went to a psychedelic space to hug my father I found after his suicide.

> I went back to California to pay property taxes, laugh, and replant roots.
>
> And when I was truly ready to honour all of it, everything that comes with the S's of grief- the silence, the swirl, the shame, the survivor, surrender, and the show up:

"I Baja-ed it"

Verb

To fully process and release something as an act of radical resilience.

Example: *"I'm happy to share that I have fully Baja-ed my last relationship and feel good about it."*

When a woman is pregnant people don't say that she is procrastinating when the child is not born each day. This year as I travelled the world writing my memoir and building a mental health start up my discomfort with not knowing how to show up fully when someone experienced loss started to take form within my mind and my consciousness. As I travelled from Los Angeles to Europe to Baja this book grew within me in a way I can only liken to a pregnancy. Fingers, toes, organs, fingernails. I was carrying it with me, but I didn't feel it was ready to find itself in the world apart from me yet. The above passage that was published on Chip Conley's "Wisdom Well" felt like a beautiful, full circle moment, but *Firs Year of Grief Club* had not yet been born. A few false sets of contractions came, but when it didn't have to happen, I didn't push. Instead, I watched the sunset and just spent a lot of time noticing and listening, and when all else failed, laughing.

Within that time, I entered a grief process I was not expecting, a professional one. And as has happened many times in the past, magic found me in Baja. Then, out of intention and hope, and a trip to do a trial run living in London, England, the book emerged. I'd like to say I went to London, cozied up, opened my laptop and boom, there was the manuscript. But it didn't emerge in the form you've enjoyed in the preceding pages until

I realized I had more grieving to do. There was no way to spare myself from the professional grief process that had to take place. Even then, I tried to go on dates, watch tv, and listen to podcasts, but something wild and wonderful occurred – there was no internet at my flat and I was hiding in plain sight in a city where I knew no one.

It was about three hours in with no internet in London that my water broke. Figuratively, of course. And this book, that has long been growing inside me, stripped of my story that will be the content of my memoir, was born. Thirteen years and 3 months, three traumatic deaths, a whirlwind of love, lack, loss and life – I found meaning that I wanted to share.

In due time, my memoir *Just To The Left Of Death* will exist to fill in my own grief journey and describe my own quest to fix what in the end can only be honoured. For now, I hope you fill the space with your own honouring — your own journey — and take my word for it that there is no wrong or right way. Just what is.

ACKNOWLEDGEMENTS

In the *Afterword*, I likened this experience to giving birth, to the best of my ability to know such a thing. This book, as all creations do, formed in my being first, before coming into the world, during my thirteen years in the Grief Club arena. Just as new parents, I would like to acknowledge each person who has had a part in seeing my two feet firmly planted on Earth today, and in securing my willingness to venture out again. In the spirit of that, and as a tribute to *Fight Club* author Chuck Palahniuk I'll share this:

“NOTHING OF ME IS ORIGINAL.
I AM THE COMBINED EFFORT
OF EVERYONE I'VE EVER KNOWN.**”**

– Chuck Palahniuk, *Invisible Monsters*

This couldn't be truer. Those who have invested in me not only surviving but thriving after my unimaginable losses, are my personal shareholders and I do everything with you in mind.

Imagining that encompasses everyone who got me to the point I felt safe enough to allow this book to be birthed, I want to acknowledge those who have made sure it is an actual physical gift that can be given to those entering Grief Club now, not just disorganized thoughts in my hyperfunctioning brain. You are the fine print to my *being:*

To My Book Team: Patti M. Hall, the Book Alchemist, Dino Marino, Dr Emee Vida Estacio.

To My Modern Elder Family for holding me and my grief: Chip Conley, Christine Sperber, Jeff Hamoui, Shelley Paxton, Cornelia Von Rittenberg, Drew Newkirk, Karen Fairty, Maura Tierney, Kay Scorah, Susan Cole, Justin Michael Williams, Jeremi Karnell, Teddi and everyone in Baja.

To the people who generously housed me so I could write but never be alone: Cornelia Von Rittenberg (London UK), Todrick Hall (Los Angeles), Cynthia & Brent MacFarlane (The Lake) and Andrew Insanally (Toronto).

To My Mother: Kimberley "Nanny Kim" Brasil who made unconditional love seem like a given growing up and from whom I have since learned it the greatest privilege of all time. To My Sisters Ashley and Autumn, Family, Friends and Champions.

To My Mentors: Jenifer Merifield, Lee Ann Daly, Chip Conley, Ryan MacCarrigan.

To My OG Grief Club friend: Andrea Bagley, you know. My Fellow Hope Monster: Jenni Thomasson who has wiped tears from eyes, blood from my face and listened without judgement to every wish, dream and hope I could come up with.

To my tethr family: Every man who shared, everyone who championed our efforts to shine an orange light and connect men around the world when so much seemed dark. Especially to my co-founders Matt Zerker and Burke White.

To my folks who sometimes literally carried me when I was unable to walk and I was unsure if I should go further in this process: Dane and Jenna Wagner, Tabitha Lupien, Corey Gayadeen, Michael Campanile, Colin Owensby, Colton Little, Adam Zwierzynski, Brooke Finney, Julia Taverner, Kat Rewilak, Franci Nicassio, Jason Henderson.

To my godchildren for being the source of light and reminding me I want to be a father: Jaxson Austin Joseph, and Walter and Wave Wagner.

To my Chickens: bock bock.

To my fellow writers who made it feel like a family affair and possible: Dr. Mandy Lehto, Tim Snell, Catherine Hammond, Cleo Stiller, Andrew Reiner, Houston Kraft, Shelley Paxton, Dr. Ranj, and David Vox.

To my mental health mascot, dog-son and number one dood: Hank Moody Jr. the Mini-Bernedoodle.

ABOUT THE AUTHOR

Addison Brasil had no intention of becoming a disruptor in the mental health and grief space. While pursuing his dream of creating stories that connect people, events in his life forced Addison to focus his full attention on surviving trauma, compounded grief, and the various outcomes of finding himself as an LGTBQ-identifying male.

Addison shows up in the world as an active, committed mental health advocate after landing *just to the left of death* three times in his 20s: losing his brother to cancer, finding his father after suicide, and surviving a fatal accident that killed a dear friend and left him relearning to walk. He attributes his ability to not only survive but thrive with PTSD and compounded grief to the presence and proliferation of community and connections in his life.

Addison co-founded and served as Head of Brand Impact for **tethr**, a worldwide men's mental health and well-being platform focused on the power of peer support. The start-up earned esteem when accelerated as a **500 Global** (formerly 500 Start Ups) portfolio company in San Francisco during the pandemic. His advocacy efforts and promotion of mental health and grief action has garnered global media acknowledgement in the New York Times and The Washington Post, and on Healthline, TMZ, and Fox News. Addison is currently writing a memoir and speaking about grief.

Addison has found meaning and purpose in building supportive communities and conscious brands in response to the losses he has faced. Following his younger brother's terminal diagnosis, he co-founded the Team Brother Bear Foundation in 2008. The organization continues to aid children and families affected by brain tumors in memory of Austin Brasil

Addison is Co-Producer and Executive Producer of the award-winning short film *The Great Artist* starring Matthew Postlethwaite, Emmy Nominee Rain Valdez, Benjamin Patterson, and Marimar Vega. Directed by Cannes Gold Lion Winner Indrani, the film will screen at the Cannes Film Festival in 2022.

Addison is regularly invited as a speaker at events and as a guest for podcasts worldwide to share his story as a lived experience expert. Addison's written work as a contributor have been featured in Los Angeles Magazine, Never Alone Blog, Chip Conley's Wisdom Well, Daddy's Digest and more.

You can find Addison on social media: @addisonbrasil and at www.addisonbrasil.com

NOTES

i   Roth, Eric. Screenplay, The Curious Cast of Benjamin Button 2008 performances by Brad Pitt, Cate Blanchett Paramount Pictures

ii   Google search results: https://www.google.com/search?q=lungs+part +of+ autonomic+nervous+system&rlz=1C5CHFA_enUS868US869 &oq=lungs+ part+of+autnomic+ne&aqs=chrome. 1.69i57j33i10i2 2i29i30.5014j0j7&sourceid=chrome&ie=UTF-8

iii   Kubler-Ross, Elisabeth. *On Death and Dying*. Scribner, 1969.

Elisabeth Kubler-Ross first identified the stages of dying in her 1969 book *On Death and Dying*. In a subsequent book, *On Grief and Grieving* (Simon & Schuster UK 2005) Kubler-Ross and co-author David Kessler adapted the stages she had observed in the dying to those the two experts had witnessed in grieving people.

iv   Kessler, David. *Finding Meaning*. Scribner, 2019.
Kessler suggests that Meaning could be a descriptor for the sixth stage, that time when we realize that grief will not end. He notes: "The five stages were never intended to be prescriptive, and this holds true for both dying and subject of this book, grieving. They are not a method of tucking messy emotions into neat packages. They don't prescribe, they describe." (page 2)

v   Devine, Megan. *It's OK That You're Not OK*. Sounds True.

vi   Gervais, D. M. (2021, April 8). *The larger the space between who a person says they are and who they actually are, the more pain that person feels when it's Exposed. be aligned. be you. pic.twitter.com/ cgyfhxnnhw*. Twitter. Retrieved January 23, 2022, from https:// twitter.com/michaelgervais/status/1379965475782864902

vii McInerny Purmont, Nora. TED Talk, 2018. "We Don't Move On From Grief, We Move Forward With It" and her book is *It's OK to Laugh (Crying is Cool Too)*. Dey Street Books, 2016.

viii Nestor, James. *Breath: The New Science of a Lost Art*. Riverhead Books, 2020.

ix Brown, Brene. (2021). Atlas of the Heart. Random House.

x https://www.npr.org/sections/health-shots/2021/12/20/1056741090/ grief-loss-holiday-brain-healing From *The Poems of Dylan Thomas*, published by New Directions. Copyright © 1952, 1953 Dylan Thomas. Copyright © 1937, 1945, 1955, 1962, 1966, 1967 the Trustees for the Copyrights of Dylan Thomas. Copyright © 1938, 1939, 1943, 1946, 1971 New Directions Publishing Corp.

xi Emotions color wheel art print. Etsy UK. (n.d.). Retrieved January 24, 2022, from https://www.etsy.com/uk/listing/990728633/emotions-color-wheel-art-print

xii *First Stage of grief: Denial*. eCondolence.com. (n.d.). Retrieved January 23, 2022, from https://www.econdolence.com/learning-center/grief-and-coping/the-stages-of-grief/first-stage-of-grief-denial/

xiii Huffington, A. S. (2017). *The sleep revolution: Transforming your life, one night at a time*. Harmony Books.

xiv Breus PhD, Michael J. http://www.thesleepdoctor.com

xv Van Der Kolk, M.D., Bessel. (2015). *The Body Keeps the Score: Brain, Mind, and Body in the Healing of Trauma*.

xvi https://www.statista.com/topics/1536/media-use/

xvi https://www.cemetery.com/learning-center/grief-and-coping/the-stages-of-grief/third-stage-of-grief-bargaining/

xvii *Setting your grief boundaries*. Whats your Grief. (2021, November 17). Retrieved January 23, 2022, from https://whatsyourgrief.com/setting-boundaries-grief-boundaries/

xviii   Kessler, David. *Finding Meaning: The Sixth Stage of Grief*

xix   Goulston, M. (2010). *Just listen: Discover the secret to getting through to absolutely anyone.* American Management Association.

xx   Lembke, A. D. (2021). *Dopamine nation: Finding balance in the age of indulgence.* Dutton Books.

xxi   *Books.* Margaret J. Wheatley. (n.d.). Retrieved January 23, 2022, from https://margaretwheatley.com/books-products/books/

xxii   *Huberman lab.* Huberman Lab Podcast Retrieved January 23, 2022, from https://hubermanlab.com/

xxiii   Mendoza, M. (n.d.). *The healing power of laughter in death and grief* ... Psychology Today . Retrieved January 23, 2022, from https://www.psychologytoday.com/us/blog/understanding-grief/201611/the-healing-power-laughter-in-death-and-grief

xxiv   Muscara, C. (2022, January 20). *Mindfulness teacher, speaker, coach.* Cory Muscara. Retrieved January 23, 2022, from https://corymuscara.com/

xxv   Goulston, M.D., Mark and Philip Goldberg. (1996). Get Out of Your Own Way: Overcoming Self-Defeating Behavior. Tarcher Pedigree.

xxvi   Van Der Kolk, Bessel.

xxvii   Bishop, G. J. (2020). *Wise as fu*k: Simple truths to guide you through the sh*tstorms of life.* Yellow Kite.

xxviii   Lembke, Anna.

xxix   Goodreads. (n.d.). *Jamie Anderson quotes (author of doctor who).* Goodreads. Retrieved January 23, 2022, from https://www.goodreads.com/author/quotes/3395454.Jamie_Anderson

xxx   McInerny, Nora. TED Talk

SELECTED ESSAYS
BY ADDISON BRASIL

LOS ANGELES MAGAZINE:

"How Robin Williams's Son
Helped Me Come to Terms with My Father's Suicide"

by Addison Brasil

https://www.lamag.com/citythinkblog/robin-williams-essay/

This story references suicide, which could distress some readers. Lifeline Network—800-773-8255—offers free emotional counseling 24 hours a day, seven days a week.

When you lose a parent to suicide you always wonder if you're going to die the same way. I imagine it's like losing a parent to Alzheimer's; no matter how hard you try, in the back of your mind you wonder if you're genetically destined to head down that same slow path. My hardest days with depression and grief give me that very feeling.

It's an unfortunate brotherhood that binds those who have survived a parent's suicide. I lost my father to suicide in 2012 and I'm often invited to speak at conferences for survivors. Last year I spoke at the Hope Rising virtual conference, founded by Kevin Hines, one of the only people who has jumped off the Golden Gate Bridge and lived. Before I gave my talk, I watched a man named Zak share the story of his own father's suicide; he was part of this brotherhood too. But Zak's story differed slightly from my own.

Zak's father was Robin Williams.

Watching Zak Williams speak, I thought to myself, *How can this happen?* In the early 1990s, my father and I laughed hysterically watching Robin Williams in *Mrs. Doubtfire*, and now I was a speaker at the same conference as his son because we both lost our larger-than-life fathers to suicide.

I felt such a deep connection to him because we both had outgoing, loving fathers whose deaths people couldn't understand. My father used to sing and dance and carry on, and he never let me see him without his hair done or properly groomed. My father couldn't be quiet for more than 30 seconds, and he playfully looked for any opportunity to join in the conversation or be silly if he could. My father did an amazing Mrs. Doubtfire impression: the whole dancing-with-the-vacuum schtick and everything.

But Zak's father *was* Mrs. Doubtfire. When Zak lost his dad, everyone felt that they'd lost Robin Williams too.

After Zak's father passed in 2014, I would use Robin as a metaphor when trying to explain to people how to understand my father and his surprising death by suicide. How could this man, who made me sing "Whoop, there it is" to get ice cream, take his own life? But when I brought up Robin Williams's suicide, they instantly understood what I meant. While my father's death sounded the alarm through my Portuguese, Catholic family and raised awareness about mental health for the people around me, Robin's death did that on a global scale. Zak had to share his loss with the world.

After Zak's talk, I wanted to reach out to him because of what we had in common. But I quickly realized that what I really wanted to say was thank you.

* * * *

Before the first time we FaceTimed, I was nervous. This wasn't the Hollywood moment I had planned on when I was a young kid inspired to move to Los Angeles. This was a connection to a movie star I had never fathomed. Then I realized Zak and I were just human beings who'd lost loved ones, fathers we thought would be there throughout our lives, when we got married and when our children were born. We were just guys who'd lost their dads.

When Zak's face popped up on my cracked iPhone screen, I have to admit, his resemblance to his father gave me goosebumps. But as he started to speak while laying back on his couch I felt my body relax as if I was speaking to someone I'd always known. Or perhaps it was just the magic of connecting with someone who had a similar life experience. The ultimate big brother, Zak is calm, reserved, and genuine. He shared openly about his addiction, recovery and jumped as quickly as possible to ask, "How can I help you, Addison?"

Neither of us dropped any magnificent truth bombs on each other and there was no hierarchy of loss, just a sense of understanding that dismantled the shyness I usually experience when first meeting someone. We met as advocates, yes, but also as everyday survivors of parental suicide.

We spoke of his being a dad, his upcoming L.A. wedding, and how we could work together to inspire more people to go beyond awareness and take mental health action. I couldn't help but make one dark joke about loss. I held my breath and waited for his response. He smiled and laughed rather than clamming up like people can tend to do when confronted with an awkward subject.

After our conversation, I was in awe of the path of self-healing he's forged, how he honors his own journey as he finds a way forward. To Zak, Robin Williams wasn't just a movie star, he was a human being, and a dad not too different from my own.

A few months later Zak attended a community event I was hosting. He sent shivers down my spine as he answered questions from men around the world and shared so openly in an effort to help others. "I've learned I am not broken," he said. "Despite experiencing traumatic events, I can recover."

We were not predisposed to die as our fathers did like I feared. No matter what we experience, the key is to accept that recovery is always possible.

There is something wildly comforting and so special about sharing space with somebody who in some way gets what you have lost. There is so much that is said without saying anything at all. So much is honored in each and every nod, and in every laugh at a weird joke that would only make sense to those with similar experiences.

I've always laughed when a doctor would ask me whether or not I was thinking about suicide. In my head I knew that anyone who found their father right after his death would think about suicide about 37 times a day.

The loss of my father and the complicated grief that accompanied it, almost led to my own suicide on a rainy summer day years later. On that day, I promised a power greater than me that if I could get through that I would go back for the others. It was in doing that, I got the opportunity to connect with Zak. I didn't have to ask Zak the questions that most people would want to know, instead, I learned something much greater. The safety and empathy I felt just by being in the presence of a peer was the greatest gift, and it's the message I want to tell the world: safe spaces lead to safety. I didn't have to do it alone, and no one else did either.

DADDY'S DIGEST WORLDWIDE:

"An Open Letter to Dads Around The World (From a Son Who Lost His Father)"

by Addison Brasil

https://daddysdigest.com/article/an-open-letter-to-dads-around-the-world-from-a-son-who-lost-his-father-to-suicide

I recently had the privilege of hosting a round table talk with fathers from the tethr for men mental health community. Two out of three of the fathers on the taping admitted they had been suicidal and just before what would have been their deaths, the thought of their sons is what stopped them. The experiences inspired them to join men's communities like **tethr**, hire coaches, do therapy and get support. So that their life was not on the shoulders of their sons. I could barely catch my breath to continue to moderate the conversation.

Why didn't my dad just think of me? Maybe he did. Maybe I wasn't enough to save him...

I want to start by saying that I am certain that my father never imagined I would be writing this letter to all of you. From the day I was born he did everything he could to provide me with all the privileges of life - security, nourishment, affection, education and a lifestyle many would dream of. It was always incredibly clear that, above all else, his priority was to keep me safe, at any cost. He spent so much time trying to shelter us from the harsh realities of life, he knew all too well. He grew up in an immigrant household that he often expressed love wasn't present in. He left home as soon as he could and had a very distant but respectful relationship with his own father.

TRIGGER WARNING:

This article discusses suicide and the experience of finding a parent after death by suicide.)

For someone who never heard 'I Love You' growing up I certainly heard it a lot from him. My dad was not a stoic macho dude who kept it all inside and told us to man up. Not at all. Think Robin Williams. Well, think Robin Williams before his death by suicide. Before the world was forced to accept the harsh reality of mental illness. The love of life, the laughter, the light that seemed like it could never go out.

It goes out sometimes. Actually quite often. Alarmingly often.

If my dad were here today here are three facts I would share with him about Mental Health from a recent article done by **CNN** with Niall Breslin and Andrew Reiner (Author of Better Boys, Better Men)

FACT 1 - "Men are far less likely than women to reach out for help when they are feeling low, according to 2019 analysis from the American Journal of Men's Health"

FACT 2 - "Data from the US Centers for Disease Control and Prevention shows that American men die by suicide at a rate three and a half times higher than women."

FACT 3 - "The prevalence of depressive symptoms being reported by adult men in the US has increased in every age group during the (COVID-19) pandemic, according to a September 2020 Boston University study."

In July of 2012, I returned home after a long road trip with friends. My dad picked me up from the airport. Except it wasn't my dad at all. The aforementioned light and laughter had gone missing. This was a quiet man wearing my dad's body. I didn't recognize the muted and somber side of a man I thought I knew better than anyone. I didn't know what to do.

For the next week and a half. My fears that something was truly wrong with my dad boiled until I couldn't hold it in anymore. He said he just wanted to sleep. That he was going through something and he didn't want his son (me) to see him this way. He would be fine after a week or so. He was adjusting to new medication. That wasn't good enough for me so we established regular check-ins. A week later on our Thursday night check-in, he told me he was feeling better. He would enjoy the weekend and then return to work on Monday.

The next morning he missed our check-in but I felt that I needed to respect his privacy as a man like he had asked and trust him. I went to see the Dark Knight. Despite all the spidey senses, all the fear, and all the discomforting thoughts swirling in my head around something still not right about my dad. I WENT TO A BATMAN MOVIE. I have worked through the guilt around this, but it serves me to share this now, to show how sure I was that my Dad would never leave me. He would never let me find him… as I did.

In the final scene of The Dark Knight created by Christopher Nolan, Commissioner Gordon said something that I will never forget. "He's the hero Gotham deserves, but not the one it needs right now. So we'll hunt him. Because he can take it. Because he's not our hero. He's a silent guardian, a watchful protector. A dark knight." I had to let my father find a way in the dark. I had to respect his process as a man. He was Batman, not me. He would be back to save me and keep me safe from this rough patch. I turned the metaphorical bat signal off in my head and called off professional help. I spent the day exhausted by inaction because I knew my dad was a superhero. I had to believe he was. He had this, he could do anything. My dad always showed up for me… always!

The next morning I found my father hanging in his apartment. There is no other way to say that. As shocked as you may have been to read that, I can tell you that's how I felt too. He was alive and then he was not.

Sometimes when I walk down the street and I see a father walking with his young son, I imagine stopping them and asking the father If I can have a word with him. I imagine a loving and accepting way that I ask the father how his mental health is? What he's doing to ensure that he will never leave his son to experience what I have?

I write this letter so your own sons, or daughters, never end up at your door with shaky hands trying to use a key that may unlock traumatic grief they will never truly recover from, but hopefully, learn to honour. (That's a different letter altogether).

My dad's greatest gift to me was one I could not give back. A fierce awareness surrounding the importance of mental health, redefining masculinity, and what it meant to be a fully feeling huMAN being. This was my inheritance and something I continually explore as I work on my first book about resilience. I hope that this letter, if nothing else, inspires each of you to take steps beyond mental health awareness and into mental health action.

Let me be that lesson to you today. So that you are never that lesson to your children. Let this open letter be a plea to allow me to pay forward my learning and encourage you to give this some thought.

My father was attractive, successful, wealthy, well-loved, respected, and cherished. None of that is a substitute for maintaining mental health and wellbeing. None of that can be traded for daily attention to your emotional health.

10 years ago I was not educated enough about men's mental health when I thought that my dad could be his own superhero for no other reason than 'he was my dad.' Today, as a co-founder of tethr for men, a writer, and a mental health advocate - I can say with absolute certainty, my dad did not have the professional support and peer community to express what he was going through to be here today. And how could he have? It didn't really exist.

Thanks to my dad I get to be part of a team every day that tries to reduce the alarming facts I gave earlier. That attempts to ease the burden of men who are so focused on caring for their families- they forget how and when to care for themselves.

Even Marvel and DC know that one superhero just doesn't cut it anymore. We need the Avengers, all of them, working together to show up to the opposing forces that exist in the 2021 landscape for fathers. Pandemics and pampers aside. You always have the power to prioritize your mental health.

I have long retired my real-life need for the bat signal, instead of at tethr, we have the orange symbol. It lets men know that they are being heard and if they need support someone is there.

Signed with sincerity,

A Son Who Lost His Father to Suicide.

WE ARE NEVER ALONE BLOG:

"Supporting PTSD and Compounded Grief Triggers"

(TRIGGER WARNING: This article discusses suicide, surviving a suicide loss, a traumatic accident, and triggers that come with PTSD and compounded Grief.)
July 21st, September 1st, March 14th.

Fresh flowers, new car smell, the taste of metal in my mouth. Headlights. Extension cords. Driving in the rain. Suicide scenes on TV/ Film. Gaslighting. Sirens. Hospitals.

Songs. Weather changes. Pain points in my body… it goes on.

The list above will most likely mean nothing to you but to me, these dates, times, experiences, and senses become similar to walking daily through an emotional minefield for me.

Since my 19th birthday, I have witnessed and survived being "Just to The Left" of three traumatic deaths of loved ones and spent almost all of my spare time, or what I like to call my second full-time job – navigating the path of three complex and compounded grief processes. And most importantly, the triggers that go along with them.

I spent years trying to "fix my grief" and my mental health. As that sentence sets in I want to fast-track you through a decade of my learning and tell you that the number one takeaway I can offer is that there is NOTHING to fix- grief is a daily relationship and your mental health is something you honor.

Let's talk about the dates I mentioned above and the experiences that have guided me away from my dreams in Hollywood to Silicon Valley where **I am a co-founder of the men's mental health app tethr** and focus on building community and encouraging emotional fitness.

Sept 1, 2008 – After a four-year battle with a brain tumour I stood at my brother's bedside with my family as he passed away.

July 21, 2012 – I went to check on my dad and found him after he had died by suicide.

March 14, 2018 – After surviving the loss of half my family, going to the ends of the earth to honour my mental health I finally felt like myself again. I went to a concert with a friend and then out to celebrate. On the way home, a fatal accident killed her and left me re-learning to walk and navigate a brain injury.

Resulting from these experiences, I have noticed a specific list of triggers that can ignite panic, fear, intense sadness, grief, or what I used to fear most – a PTSD flashback. For me, grief isn't just about losing a person or a life. Grief can result from the loss of anything meaningful to you a partner, a job, access, a major life transition or change. I have witnessed many friends and family grieving the lifestyle changes that the pandemic brought on.

I am not a doctor and am not a mental health professional. In fact, I have purposely stayed in a peer position. I'm just one of the guys, a human being with the divine right for healing as an exploration for everyone. The following 5 takeaways around triggers are from my perspective and I hope they can serve you in some way. I have not watched from above or studied grief academically, as Brene Brown and Theodore Roosevelt would say – I have been in the area. I have become an expert in my lived experience with the hope of empowering others to do the same.

ACKNOWLEDGE YOUR TRIGGERS, RATHER THAN TRYING TO DISMISS THEM

It seems too simple, but I often would avoid my triggers and their aftermath entirely. By Acknowledging them and the feelings that came up for me as a result I was able to not just be reactive to them but become proactive. When I notice a trigger coming up – the smell of fresh flowers for example I now breathe into it and lovingly acknowledge what comes up physically, mentally, and emotionally

MAKE A LIST OF YOUR TRIGGERS

Much like I did to start this article, arm yourself with the list. I have come to learn that my grief is not going anywhere. It is a daily relationship and something I honor every day based on how I'm feeling and what triggers the next wave of memories, emotions, and even flashbacks.

My list exists as a source of knowledge and power for me. I don't avoid the items listed at all costs or fear them – instead, I try to approach them by coming up with a little more self-care and radical acceptance. Consider what your positive triggers are, and neutral triggers too so you can use them in your mental health tool belt to ground yourself.

Obviously, I can't avoid fresh flowers, rain, and headlights if I want to live a normal life. Each interaction allows me to be a little bit more resilient.

GET THE HELP YOU NEED, WHEN YOU NEED IT.

Part of the process is figuring out what truly serves you, and what will ultimately allow you to heal within your relationship with grief and triggers, is getting help. Whether it's naturopathic, psychedelic, psychiatric or trusted peers in a safe space – I encourage you to begin seeking help as an undeniable strength. Community and compassion are the reasons I have survived my own suicidality in the wake of my losses and injuries.

CONSUME CONTENT CONSCIOUSLY (NETFLIX AND CHILL, LIKE ACTUALLY STAY CHILL)

We have all had that moment when watching a film where we know something from our own life might be triggered by the next scene. Whether it's our spidey senses telling us things are too calm and there's about to be an accident or a gut feeling that we are about to witness a sexual assault or a character's suicide. Trust that.

Many friends know that viewing a horrific accident or a suicide can really set me back. And they know because I have acknowledged the triggers and shared them. I will get texts from friends that say a tv show title, an episode number, and sometimes even a minute count. I instantly know what it means.

Being prepared by getting a heads up or researching trigger warnings before a Netflix binge is proactive.

CREATE NEW EXPERIENCES WITH YOUR TRIGGERS

Over the past six months, after ten years of many mental health modalities, I felt grounded and safe enough to begin to rewire my neural pathways in response to my triggers. Essentially, I have been purposely exposing myself to my triggers and anchoring new memories to them.

Here are some examples:

- Whenever something very positive is happening I will go back and listen to an old song that I love but that also reminds me of a triggering event. I bring the song forward with me into the new memory and detach it from being a direct correlation to a past event.

- Plan a trip where the triggers will exist but the environment changes. I recently went to Positano in Italy. It was an amazing experience because the sound of the sirens is different, so I was able to acknowledge that sirens exist without being an attack on my nervous system. Additionally, part of what makes Positano one of the most beautiful places on earth is the nature that surrounds the hillside town. I made a point of stopping to smell the fresh flowers every day. Flowers aren't just in funeral homes, they are also an essential part of my new favorite place in the world.

- I made a lot of silly and fun trips to Home Depot to desensitize myself to household items that remind me of my father's suicide. My friends who tagged along had no idea that I was spending extra time in certain aisles to do this.

- Lastly, my brother's name was Austin – and if that name came up it usually meant that we were talking about my brother who passed, brain tumors, or something that would be triggering. As I write this, I am currently working remotely from Austin, Texas. His name is everywhere and I can find peace in knowing that we can co-exist and I love seeing it and hearing it without the direct correlation.

I share this in an effort to connect. I can remember countless times in my grief process where I felt unnecessarily isolated and alone. While every grief process is significantly different and we all have different triggers from trauma and life experiences, I find peace in knowing experientially I am not alone.

TALES THAT TETHR:

Addison Brasil's Story of Acceptance and Authenticity for National Coming Out Day

Welcome to tales that tethr, a series written by and for the tethr community. If you'd like to share your own story of strength and support, click here. Today we're honored to share Addison's story. A tale for #NationalComingOutDay.

Our dinner table was long and brown solid wood. It had been passed down, re-stained, and shared by families before us. It wasn't pristine and it didn't seem like something in a Stepford museum of interior design. My mother or as she wants to be called one-day "Glamma" loved that table for all of those reasons. She loved that our second-grade homework was carved into it from the times we worked at it without anything under our lined paper. She liked the scuff marks that lovingly marked my brother's seat at the table from his years with a metal back brace. That table was safe for us to nurture ourselves, discuss, disagree, spill milk and live.

Our table has come to represent so much more to me. To my surprise, I have met so many people in my life that were unaccepted or even outcast for finding love. Whether it be to someone of the same gender identity or an "unsuitable choice" - it is lost on me that parents would forbid the one thing that can carry us through it all - love.

In our house we just had dinner. And at our table everyone was welcome. You brought a girl to dinner - we ate dinner. You brought a boy to dinner - we ate dinner. You came alone - we ate damn dinner. You brought someone who identified as non-binary, the only question you had was whether or not they could pass the mashed potatoes.

As I meet more people who did not share this upbringing - I wish everyone who never had a table like this that allowed them to just "be" while they safely refueled and nurtured their minds could sit at this table now.

No longer in our family- I hope whoever sits at it now rubs their fingers on the markings our family left on it and feels the love-based platform it was for us all.

It was for us to find freedom and even fluidity in our lives and how we love.

My spot was on the right-hand side at the end of three chairs. And eventually at the head of the table. I grew up at that table, but also had every opportunity to be a kid.

Homework. Drawing. Funny stories and jokes. Hard conversations. Frustrations over spilled milk and who made dinner by when. Beer Pong. Hours of games. We had our first Board meeting ever at that table. And it was circled by love at the wake of my brother and father. Anyone was welcome. As I said, it was a platform for love and a support group for fear. Not just a table.

What's kind of table will you have in your home? Will you be able to allow your children so much more than a piece of furniture. I never thought furniture could be story-driven - able to connect us to our past and guide us in shaping our future.

And to my future children; I can't wait to see whom you bring to dinner, to love them as you do...to learn and grow from them. I hope you feel our table was more than just a place to eat- but a safe space to digest, refuel and connect.

Made in the USA
Columbia, SC
17 March 2022

57786429R10115